MORE CHUCKLES

1001 POLITICALLY INCORRECT JOKES

Kerry O'Seanhan

INFINITY
PUBLISHING.COM

ISBN 0-7414-5708-3

Published by:

INFINITY
PUBLISHING.COM

1094 New DeHaven Street, Suite 100
West Conshohocken, PA 19428-2713
Info@buybooksontheweb.com
www.buybooksontheweb.com
Toll-free (877) BUY BOOK
Local Phone (610) 941-9999
Fax (610) 941-9959

Printed in the United States of America

Published November 2009

Dedication

This book is dedicated to Omar, Robert, Grace, Lucy and Ken. Without these people, this book would never have been written.

FOREWORD

The title of this book says it all: CHUCKLE! It is often said that laughter is the best medicine. If this is true, then you are in for a lot of medicine. People need to take life less seriously and learn to relax and get along. The best way to do that is to learn to laugh. You must first learn to laugh at yourself before you can laugh at the world. There are jokes in here that are sure to offend some people but given the fact that I'm not politically correct, I don't care. There are ethnic jokes, men and women bashing, lawyer, doctor and religious jokes. There are sex jokes, gay and straight jokes, Black, White, Asian and every other type of joke you can imagine. However, this book is fair and balanced, everybody gets teased. People often tell jokes within a certain group about another group such as blacks tell jokes about white or whites about blacks. These jokes have been passed around for many years but I have the poor taste to compile them all in one place. My intent is not to be hurtful to anybody, but to teach how to laugh at yourself and then at others. Everything in life is easier and better when you're smiling. Enjoy this book and remember to take all of these jokes with a smile and try not to be too offended

An old man goes to the Wizard to ask him if he can remove a curse he has been living with for the last 40 years. The Wizard says, “Maybe, but you will have to tell me the exact words that were used to put the curse on you.” The old man says without hesitation, “I now pronounce you man and wife.”

Two Reasons Why It's So Hard To Solve A Redneck Murder

1. All the DNA is the same.
2. There are no dental records.

A blonde calls Delta Airlines and asks, “Can you tell me how long it'll take to fly from San Francisco to New York City?” The agent replies, “Just a minute...” “Thank you,” the blonde says, and hangs up.

This guy has been sitting in a bar all night, staring at a blonde wearing the tightest pants he's ever seen. Finally his curiosity gets the best of him, so he walks over and asks, “How do you get into those pants?” The young woman looks him over and replies, “Well, you could start by buying me a drink.”

Moe: “My wife got me to believe in religion.”
Joe: “Really?”
Moe: “Yeah. Until I married her I didn't believe in hell.”

Three men are sitting stiffly side-by-side on a long plane flight. After 30 minutes the man in the window seat suddenly says distinctly and confidently in a low voice: “General, United States Army, married, two sons, both surgeons.” After another half hour the man on the aisle reveals through a tight lipped smile: “General, United States Air Force, married, two sons, both judges.” Yet another 30 minutes passes before the one in the middle seat with eyes twinkling, loudly proclaims: “Retired Gunny Sergeant, United States Marine Corps, never married, two sons, both generals.”

A guy sitting at a bar at Heathrow Airport noticed a really beautiful woman sitting next to him. He thought to himself: “Wow, she's so gorgeous she must be an off duty flight attendant. But which airline does she work for?” Hoping to make her acquaintance, he leaned towards her and uttered the Delta slogan: “Love to fly and it shows?” She gave him a blank, confused stare and he immediately thought to himself: “Damn, she doesn't work for Delta.” A moment later, another slogan popped into his head. He leaned towards her again, “A great way to fly?” She gave him the same confused look. He mentally kicked himself, and scratched Singapore Airlines off the list. Next he tried the Thai Airways slogan: “Smooth as Silk.” This time the woman turned on him, “What the fuck do you want?” The man smiled, then slumped back in his chair, and said “Ahhhh, American Airlines!”

An Afghan curse: “May the fleas of a thousand Afghan camels infest the crotch of the person who screws up your day and may their arms be too short to scratch.”

A man is recovering from surgery when a nurse asks him how he is feeling. “I'm O. K. but I didn't like the four-letter-word the doctor used in surgery,” he answered. “What did he say,” asked the nurse. “OOPS!”

<u>10 DOG PEEVES ABOUT HUMANS</u>

1. Blaming your farts on me... not funny... not very funny at all!
2. Yelling at me for barking... I’M A FRIGGIN’ DOG YOU IDIOT!
3. Taking me for a walk, then not letting me check stuff out. Exactly whose walk is this anyway?
4. Any trick that involves balancing food on my nose... stop it!
5. Any haircut that involves bows or ribbons. Now you know why we chew your stuff up when you're not home.
6. The sleight of hand, fake fetch throw. You fooled a dog! What a proud moment for the top of the food chain.

7. Taking me to the vet for "the big snip", then acting surprised when I freak out every time we go back.
8. Getting upset when I sniff the crotches of your guests. Sorry, but I haven't quite mastered that handshake thing yet.
9. How you act disgusted when I lick myself. Look, we both know the truth, you're just jealous.
10. Dog sweaters. HELLO!! Have you noticed the fur?

From a strictly mathematical viewpoint it goes like this: What makes 100%? What does it mean to give MORE than 100%? Ever wonder about those people who say they are giving more than 100%? We have all been to those meetings where someone wants you to give over 100%. How about achieving 103%? What makes up 100% in life? Here's a little mathematical formula that might help you answer these questions:

If: A B C D E F G H I J K L M N O P Q R S T U V W X Y Z is represented as: 1 2 3 4 5 6 7 8 9 10 11 12 13 14 15 16 17 18 19 20 21 22 23 24 25 26. Then:
H-A-R-D-W-O-R-K or 8+1+18+4+23+15+18+11 = 98%
and K-N-O-W-L-E-D-G-E or 11+14+15+23+12+5+4+7+5 = 96%
But, A-T-T-I-T-U-D-E or 1+20+20+9+20+21+4+5 = 100%
And, B-U-L-L-S-H-I-T or 2+21+12+12+19+8+9+20 = 103%
AND, look how far ass kissing will take you.
A-S-S-K-I-S-S-I-N-G or 1+19+19+11+9+19+19+9+14+7 = 118%
So, one can then conclude with mathematical certainty that while Hard Work and Knowledge will get you close and Attitude will get you there, it's Bullshit and Ass kissing will put you over the top.

<u>26 New Office Words, Terms and Definitions added to the Dictionary</u>

1. Assmosis - The process by which some people seem to absorb success and advancement by kissing up to the boss.

2. Blamestorming - Sitting around in a group discussing why a deadline was missed or a project failed and who was responsible.

3. Seagull Manager - A manager, who flies in, makes a lot of noise, craps over everything, and then leaves.

4. Salmon Day - The experience of spending an entire day swimming upstream only to get screwed and die in the end.

5. Irritainment - Entertainment and media spectacles that are annoying but you find yourself unable to stop watching them. The O.J. trials were a prime example.

6. Chainsaw Consultant - An outside expert brought in to reduce the employee head count, leaving the brass with clean hands.

7. Career Limiting Move (CLM) - Used among microserfs to describe an ill-advised activity. Trashing your boss while he or she is within earshot is a serious CLM.

8. Adminisphere - The rarefied organizational layers beginning just above rank and file. Decisions that fall from the adminisphere are often profoundly inappropriate or irrelevant to the problems they were designed to solve.

9. Flight Risk - Used to describe employees who are suspected of planning to leave the company or department soon.

10. "404" - Someone who's clueless. From the World Wide Web error message "404-URL Not Found" meaning that the requested web page could not be located. Used as in: "Don't bother asking him...he's 404, man."

11. Generica - Features of the American landscape that are exactly the same no matter where one is, such as fast food joints, strip malls, subdivisions. Used as in: “We were so lost in Generica that I forgot what city we were in.”

12. Ohno-Second - That minuscule fraction of time in which you realize that you've just made a BIG mistake.

13. Percussive Maintenance - The fine art of whacking the crap out of an electronic device to get it to work again.

14. Umfriend - A sexual relation of dubious standing or concealed intimate relationship, as in “This is Dylan, my ...um...friend.”

15. Body Nazis - Hard-core exercise and weightlifting fanatics who look down on anyone who doesn't work out obsessively.

16. Cube Farm - An office filled with cubicles.

17. Idea Hamsters - People who always seem to have their idea generators running.

18. SITCOMs - What yuppies turn into when they have children and one of them stops working to stay home with the kids. Stands for “Single Income, Two Children, and Oppressive Mortgage”.

19. Mouse Potato - The on-line, wired generation's answer to the couch potato.

20. Prairie Dogging - When someone yells or drops something loudly in a cube farm, and people's heads pop up over the walls to see what's going on.

21. Starter Marriage - A short-lived first marriage that ends in divorce with no kids, no property and no regrets.

22. Stress Puppy - A person who seems to thrive on being stressed out and whiny.

23. Swiped Out - An ATM or credit card that has been rendered useless because the magnetic strip is worn away from extensive use.

24. Alpha Geek - The most knowledgeable, technically proficient person in an office or work group.

25. G.O.O.D. Job - A "Get-Out-Of-Debt" job. A well-paying job people take in order to pay off their debts, one that they will quit as soon as they are solvent again.

26. Yuppie Food Stamps - The ubiquitous $20 bills spewed out of ATMs everywhere. Often used when trying to split the bill after a meal: "We owe $8 each, but all anybody's got are yuppie food stamps."

Aviation Facts:

Takeoffs are optional. Landings are mandatory.

If you push the stick forward, the houses get bigger, if you pull the stick back they get smaller. (Unless you keep pulling the stick back then they get bigger again.)

Flying is not dangerous; crashing is dangerous.

It's better to be down here wishing you were up there, than up there wishing you were down here.

The propeller is just a big fan in the front of the plane to keep the pilot cool. Make it stop; then watch the pilot break out into a sweat.

It's best to keep the pointed end going forward as much as possible.

The only time you have too much fuel is when you're on fire.

The probability of survival is equal to the angle of arrival. Always remember you fly an airplane with your head, not your hands.

Learn from the mistakes of others. You won't live long enough to make all of them yourself.

There are three simple rules for making a smooth landing. Unfortunately, no one knows what they are.

It's easy to make a small fortune in aviation. You start with a large fortune.

Try to keep the number of your landings equal to the number of your takeoffs.

You cannot propel yourself forward by patting yourself on the back.

There are old pilots, and there are bold pilots, but there are no old, bold, pilots!

Gravity never looses, the best you can hope for is a draw!

Two guys were roaring down the road on a motorcycle when the driver slowed up and pulled over. His leather jacket had a broken zipper, and he told his friend, “I can't drive anymore with the air hitting me in the chest like that.” “Just put the jacket on backwards.” His friend advised. They continued down the road but around the next bend, they lost control and wiped out. A nearby farmer came upon the accident and ran to call the police. They asked him, “Are they showing any signs of life?” “Well,” the farmer explained, “the driver was until I turned his head around the right way!”

A little old lady wanted to join a biker club. She knocked on the door of a local biker club and a big, hairy, bearded biker with tattoos all over his arms answers the door. She proclaims "I want to join your biker club." The guy was amused and told her that she needed to meet certain biker requirements before she was allowed to join. So the biker asks her "You have a bike?" The little old lady says "Yeah, that's my Harley over there" and points to a Harley parked in the driveway. The biker asks her "Do you smoke?" The little old lady says "Yeah, I smoke. I smoke 4 packs of cigarettes a day and a couple of cigars while I'm shooting pool." The biker is impressed and asks "Well, have you ever been picked up by the Fuzz?" The little old lady says "No, never been picked up by the fuzz, but I've been swung around by my nipples a few times."

Do you keep falling asleep in meetings and seminars? What about those long and boring conference calls? Here's a way to change all of that:

1. Before (or during) your next meeting, seminar, or conference call, prepare yourself by drawing a square. I find that 5"x5" is a good size. Divide the card into columns-five across and five down. That will give you 25 one-inch blocks.

2. Write one of the following words/phrases in each block: - synergy - strategic fit - core competencies -best practice - bottom line - revisit - expeditious - out of the loop - benchmark - value-added - proactive - win-win -24/7 - think outside the box - fast track - result-driven - leverage - empower (or empowerment) - knowledge base - mind set - at the end of the day - touch base - paradigm - game plan

3. Check off the appropriate block when you hear one of those words/phrases.

4. When you get five blocks horizontally, vertically, or

diagonally, stand up and shout "BULLSHIT!"

Two nuns are ordered to paint a room in the convent, and the last instruction of the Mother Superior is that they must not get even a drop of paint on their habits. After conferring about this for a while, the two nuns decide to lock the door of the room, strip off their habits, and paint in the nude. In the middle of the project, there comes a knock at the door. "Who is it?", calls one of the nuns. "Blind man," replies a voice from the other side of the door. The two nuns look at each other and deciding that no harm can come from letting a blind man into the room, they open the door. "Nice boobs," says the man, "where do you want the blinds?"

Blondes.... A few days ago I was having some work done at my local garage. A blonde came in and asked for a seven-hundred-ten. We all looked at each other and another customer asked, "What is a seven-hundred-ten?" She replied, "You know, the little piece in the middle of the engine. I have lost it and need a new one." The mechanic gave her a pen and paper and asked her to draw a picture of the piece. She drew a circle and in the middle of it wrote 710. He then took her over to another car, which had its hood up and asked, "Is there a 710 on this car?" She pointed and said, "Of course, it's right there." The mechanic noticed the cap and laughingly explained to the blond that it did not say 710 it said OIL.

An Irishman, a Mexican, and a blond guy were doing construction work on scaffolding on the 20th floor of a building. They were eating lunch, and the Irishman said, "Corned beef and cabbage! If I get corned beef and cabbage one more time for lunch I'm going to jump off this building." The Mexican opened his lunch box and exclaimed, "Burritos again! If I get burritos one more time I'm going to jump off, too." The blond opened his lunch and said, "Bologna again. If I get a bologna sandwich one more time I'm jumping too." Next day the Irishman opens his lunch box, sees corned beef and cabbage, and jumps to his death. The Mexican opens his lunch, sees a burrito and jumps too. The blond opens his lunch, sees the bologna, and jumps to his death also. At the funeral The Irishman's wife is weeping. She says, "If I'd known how really tired he was of corned beef and cabbage I never would have given it to him again! The Mexican's wife also weeps and says, "I could have given him tacos or enchiladas! I didn't realize he hated burritos so much." Everyone turned and stared at the blonde's wife. "Hey, don't look at me" she said. "He makes his own lunch."

Q. What is Bush's opinion on Roe vs. Wade?
A. He says it doesn't matter how people get out of New Orleans.

A blonde went into a world wide message center to send a message to her mother overseas. When the man told her it would cost $300, she exclaimed: "But I don't have any money. But I'd do anything to get a message to my mother". The man arched an eyebrow "Anything?" he asked. "Yes, yes, anything" the blonde promised. "Well then, just follow me" said the man as he walked towards the next room. The blonde did as she was told and followed the man. "Come in and close the door" the man said. She did. He then said "Now get on your knees". She did. "Now take down my zipper". She did. "Now go ahead ...take it out..." he said. She reached in and grabbed it with both hands ...then paused. The man closed his eyes and whispered "Well... go ahead". The blonde slowly brought her mouth closer to it and while holding it close to her lips, tentatively said....."Hello, mom can you hear me?"

Hung Chow calls into work and says, "Hey, boss I no come work today, I really sick. Got headache, stomachache and legs hurt, I no come work." The boss says, "You know Hung Chow, I really need you today. When I feel like this I go to my wife and tell her to give me sex. That makes everything better and I go to work. You try that." Two hours later Hung Chow calls again. "Boss, I do what you say and I feel great. I be at work soon. You got nice house."

<u>Actually Taken From Classified Ad's In Newspapers:</u>
FREE YORKSHIRE TERRIER. 8 years old. Hateful little dog. Bites.

FREE PUPPIES: 1/2 Cocker Spaniel, 1/2 sneaky neighbor's dog.

FREE PUPPIES... Part German Shepherd, part stupid dog.

GERMAN SHEPHERD 85 lbs. Neutered. Speaks German. Free

FOUND: DIRTY WHITE DOG. Looks like a rat ... been out awhile. Better be reward.

COWS, CALVES NEVER BRED... Also 1 gay bull for sale.

NORDIC TRACK $300 Hardly used, call Chubby.

GEORGIA PEACHES, California grown - 89 cents lb.

NICE PARACHUTE: Never opened - used once.

FOR SALE BY OWNER: Complete set of Encyclopedia Britannica. 45 volumes. Excellent condition. Best offer. No longer needed. Got married last month. Wife knows everything.

After numerous rounds of "We don't even know if Saddam is still alive," Saddam decided to send George W. a letter in his own writing to let him know that he is still in the game. Bush opened the letter and it appeared to contain a coded message: "370HSSV 0773H". George W. couldn't figure it out so he typed it out and emailed it to Colin Powell. Colin and his aides had no clue either so they sent it to the CIA. No one could solve it so it went to the NSA and then to MIT and

NASA and the Secret Service ... the list got longer and longer. Eventually they asked Mossad in Israel for help. Captain Moshe Pippick took one look at it and replied: "Tell the President that he is looking at the message upside down."

How many dogs does it take to change a light bulb?

1. Golden Retriever: The sun is shining, the day is young, we've got our whole lives ahead of us, and you're inside worrying about a stupid burned out bulb?

2. Border Collie: Just one. And then I'll replace any wiring that's not up to code.

3. Dachshund: You know I can't reach that stupid lamp

4. Rottweiler: Make me.

5. Boxer: Who cares? I can still play with my squeaky toys in the dark.

6. Lab: Oh, me, me!!!!! Pleeeeeeeeeze let me change the light bulb! Can I? Can I? Huh? Huh? Huh? Can I? Pleeeeeeeeeze, please, please, please!

7. Greyhound: It isn't moving. Who cares?

8. Jack Russell Terrier: I'll just pop it in while I'm bouncing off the walls and furniture.

9. Old English Sheep Dog: Light bulb? I'm sorry, but I don't see a light bulb!

10. Cocker Spaniel: Why change it? I can still pee on the carpet in the dark.

11. Chihuahua: Yo quiero Taco Bulb. Or "We don't need no stinking light bulb."

12. German Shepherd: I'll change it as soon as I've led these people from the dark, check to make sure I haven't missed any, and make just one more perimeter patrol to see that no one has tried to take advantage of the situation.

13. Australian Shepherd: First, I'll put all the light bulbs in a little circle…

A woman was having a passionate affair with an inspector from a pest control company. One afternoon, they were carrying on in the bedroom together when her husband arrived home unexpectedly. "Quick," said the woman to her lover, "into the closet!" and she pushed him in the closet, stark naked. The husband however became suspicious and after a search of the bedroom discovered the man in the closet. "Who are you?" he asked him. "I'm an inspector from Bugs-B-Gone," said the exterminator. "What are you doing here?" the husband asked. "I'm investigating a complaint about an infestation of moths." the man replied. "And where are your clothes?" asked the husband. The man looked down at himself and said.... "Those little bastards".

Once upon a time, in a land far away, a beautiful, independent, self-assured princess happened upon a frog as she sat, contemplating ecological issues on the shores of an unpolluted pond in a verdant meadow near her castle. The frog hopped into the princess' lap and said: Elegant Lady, I was once a handsome prince, until an evil witch cast a spell upon me. One kiss from you, however, and I will turn back into the dapper, young prince that I am and then, my sweet, we can marry and setup housekeeping in your castle with my mother, where you can prepare my meals, clean my clothes, bear my children, and forever feel grateful and happy doing so. That night, as the princess dined sumptuously on a repast of lightly sautéed frog legs seasoned in a white wine and onion cream sauce, she chuckled and thought to herself.......I don't freaking think so.

<u>France Quotes From Famous People</u>

France has neither winter nor summer nor morals. Apart from these drawbacks it is a fine country" ---Mark Twain

"I would rather have a German division in front of me than a French one behind me." --- General George S. Patton

"Going to war without France is like going deer hunting without your accordion." --Norman Schwarzkopf

"We can stand here like the French, or we can do something about it." ---- Marge Simpson

"As far as I'm concerned, war always means failure" --- Jacques Chirac, President of France

"As far as France is concerned, you're right." ---Rush Limbaugh,

"The only time France wants us to go to war is when the German Army is sitting in Paris sipping coffee." --- Regis Philbin

"The French are a smallish, monkey-looking bunch and not dressed any better, on average, than the citizens of Baltimore. True, you can sit outside in Paris and drink little cups of coffee, but why this is more stylish than sitting inside and drinking large glasses of whiskey I don't know." --- P.J O'Rourke (1989)

"You know, the French remind me a little bit of an aging actress of the 1940s who was still trying to dine out on her looks but doesn't have the face for it." ---John McCain, U.S. Senator from Arizona

"You know why the French don't want to bomb Saddam Hussein? Because he hates America, he loves mistresses and wears a beret. He is French, people." --Conan O'Brien

The next time there is a war the loser has to keep France". --Anonymous

"I don't know why people are surprised that France won't help us get Saddam out of Iraq. After all, France wouldn't help us get the Germans out of France!" ---Jay Leno

"The last time the French asked for 'more proof' it came marching into Paris under a German flag." --David Letterman

Two guys were discussing popular family trends on sex, marriage, and values. Stu said, "I didn't sleep with my wife before we got married, did you?" Leroy replied, "I'm not sure, what was her maiden name?"

A little boy went up to his father and asked: "Dad, where did all of my intelligence come from?" The father replied, "Well son, you must have got it from your mother, cause I still have mine."

"Mr. Clark, I have reviewed this case very carefully," the divorce court Judge said, "and I've decided to give your wife $775 a week." "That's very fair, your honor" the husband said. "And every now and then I'll try to send her a few bucks myself."

A doctor examined a woman, took the husband aside, and said, "I don't like the looks of your wife at all." "Me neither doc," said the husband. "But she's a great cook and really good with the kids."

While shopping for vacation clothes, my husband and I passed a display of bathing suits. It had been at least ten years and twenty pounds since I had even considered buying a bathing suit, so I sought my husband's advice. "What do you think?" I asked, "Should I get a bikini or an all-in-one?" "Better get a bikini," he replied. "You'd never get it all in one."

A city boy, Kenny, moved to the country and bought a donkey from an old farmer for $100.00. The farmer agreed to deliver the donkey the next day. The next day the farmer drove up and said, “Sorry son, but I have some bad news, the donkey died.” Kenny replied, “Well then, just give me my money back.” The farmer said, “Can't do that. I went and spent it already.” Kenny said, “OK then, just unload the donkey.” The farmer asked, “What ya gonna do with him?” Kenny: “I'm going to raffle him off.” Farmer: “You can't raffle off a dead donkey!” Kenny: Sure I can, watch me. I just won't tell anybody he is dead.” A month later the farmer met up with Kenny and asked, “What happened with that dead donkey?” Kenny replied, “I raffled him off. I sold 500 tickets at two dollars a piece and made a profit of $898.00.” Farmer: “Didn't anyone complain?” Kenny: “Just the guy who won. So I gave him his two dollars back.” Kenny grew up and eventually became the chairman of Enron.

<u>Dead Horse Wisdom</u>
The tribal wisdom of the Dakota Indians, passed on from one generation to the next says that “When you discover that you are riding a dead horse, the best strategy is to dismount.” However, today, other strategies are used by the Government such as:

1. Buying a stronger whip.
2. Changing riders.
3. Appointing a committee to study the horse.
4. Arranging to visit other countries to see how other cultures ride dead horses.
5. Lowering the standards so that dead horses can be included.
6. Reclassifying the dead horse as living impaired.
7. Hiring outside contractors to ride the dead horse.
8. Harnessing several dead horses together to increase speed.
9. Providing additional funding and/or training to increase dead horses' performance.

10. Doing a productivity study to see if lighter riders would improve the dead horse's performance.
11. Declaring that as the dead horse does not have to be fed, it is less costly, carries lower overhead and therefore contributes substantially more to the bottom line of the economy than do some other horses.
12. Promoting the dead horse to a supervisory position.
13. Rewriting the expected performance requirements for all horses.

The husband is reading the morning paper when his wife asks; "What would you do if I died, would you get married again?"
HUSBAND: "Definitely not!"
WIFE: "Why not don't you like being married?"
HUSBAND: "Of course I do."
WIFE: "Then why wouldn't you remarry?"
HUSBAND: "Okay, I'd get married again."
WIFE: "You would? (with a hurtful look on her face).
HUSBAND: (Makes audible groan).
WIFE: "Would you live in our house?"
HUSBAND: "Sure, it's a great house."
WIFE: "Would you sleep with her in our bed?"
HUSBAND: "Where else would we sleep?"
WIFE: "Would you let her drive my car?"
HUSBAND: "Probably, it is almost new."
WIFE: "Would you replace my pictures with hers?"
HUSBAND: "That would seem like the proper thing to do"
WIFE: "Would she use my golf clubs?"
HUSBAND: "No, she's left-handed."
WIFE: - - Silence - -
HUSBAND: "Shit!"

WHAT GREETING CARDS DON'T SAY BUT SHOULD!

Happy Birthday!
You look great for your age.
Almost lifelike!
My tire was thumping.

I thought it was flat
When I looked at the tire...
I noticed your cat.....Sorry!
Heard your wife left you,
How upset you must be.
But don't fret about it...
She moved in with me.

Looking back over the years
That we've been together,
I can't help but wonder...
"What the hell was I thinking?"

Congratulations on your wedding day!
Too bad no one likes your husband.

How could two people as beautiful as you
Have such an ugly baby?

I've always wanted to have
Someone to hold, someone to love.
After having met you ..
I've changed my mind.

I must admit, you brought religion into my life.
I never believed in Hell until I met you.

As the days go by, I think of how lucky I am...
That you're not here to ruin it for me.

Happy Birthday, Uncle Dad!
(Available only in Tennessee, Kentucky & West Virginia)

Congratulations on your promotion.
Before you go...
Would you like to take this knife out of my back?
You'll probably need it again.

When we were together
You always said you'd die for me.
Now that we've broken up,
I think it's time you kept your promise.

We have been friends for a very long time ...
Let's say we stop?

I'm so miserable without you
It's almost like you're here.

Congratulations on your new bundle of joy.
Did you ever find out who the father was?

Your friends and I wanted to do
Something special for your birthday.
So we're having you put to sleep.

So your daughter's a hooker,
And it spoiled your day.
Look at the bright side,
It's really good pay.

Men Are Just Happier People-- What do you expect from such simple creatures? Your last name stays put. The garage is all yours. Wedding plans take care of themselves. Chocolate is just another snack. You can be President. You can never be pregnant. You can wear a white T-shirt to a water park. You can wear NO shirt to a water park. Car mechanics tell you the truth. The world is your urinal. You never have to drive to another gas station restroom because this one is just too icky. You don't have to stop and think of which way to turn a nut on a bolt. Same work, more pay. Wrinkles add character. Wedding dress $5000, Tux rental-$100. People never stare at your chest when you're talking to them. The occasional well-rendered belch is practically expected. New shoes don't cut, blister, or mangle your feet. One mood all the time. Phone conversations are over in 30 seconds flat. You know stuff about tanks. A five-day vacation requires only one suitcase. You can open all your own jars. You get extra credit for the slightest act of thoughtfulness. If someone forgets to invite you, he or she can still be your friend. Your underwear is $8.95 for a three-pack. You almost never have strap problems in public. You are unable to see wrinkles in your clothes. Everything on your face stays its original color. The same hairstyle lasts for years, maybe decades. You only have to shave your face and neck. You can play with toys all your life. Your belly usually hides your big hips. One wallet and one pair of shoes one color for all seasons. You can wear shorts no matter how your legs look. You can "do" your nails with a pocket knife. You have freedom of choice concerning growing a mustache. You can do Christmas shopping for 25 relatives on December 24 in 25 minutes. No wonder men are happier.

John O'Reilly hoisted his beer and said, "Here's to spending the rest of me life, between the legs of me wife!" That won him the top prize at the pub for the best toast of the night! He went home and told his wife, Mary, "I won the prize for the best toast of the night." She said, "Aye, did ye now. And what was your toast?" John said, "Here's to spending the rest of me life, sitting in church beside me wife. "Oh, that is very nice indeed, John!" Mary said. The next day, Mary ran into one of John's drinking buddies on the street corner. The man chuckled leeringly and said, "John won the prize the other night at the pub with a toast about you, Mary." She said, "Aye, he told me, and I was a bit surprised meself. You know, he's only been there twice! Once he fell asleep, an the other time I had to pull him by the ears to make him come"

There were three desperately ill men met with their doctor one day to discuss their options. One was an alcoholic, one was a chain smoker, and one was a homosexual. The doctor, addressing all three of them, said, "If any of you indulge in your vices one more time, you will surely die." The men left the doctor's office, each convinced that he would never again indulge himself in his vice. While walking toward the subway for their return trip to the suburbs, they passed a bar. The alcoholic, hearing the loud music and smelling the ale, could not stop himself. His buddies went with him into the bar, where he had a shot of whiskey. No sooner had he replaced the shot glass on the bar, he fell off his stool, stone cold dead. His companions, really shocked, left the bar and realized how seriously they must take the doctor's words. As they walked along, they came upon a cigarette butt lying on the ground, still burning. The homosexual looked at the chain smoker and said, “If you bend over to pick that up, we're both dead.”

A construction worker who was on the 6th floor of a building needed a handsaw. He spots another worker on the ground floor and yells down to him, but the other worker can't hear him. The worker on the 6th floor tries some sign language. He pointed to his eye, meaning “I”, pointed to his knee, meaning “need”, and then moved his hand back and forth in a hand saw motion. The guy on the ground floor pulls down his pants, whips out his dick and starts masturbating. The worker on the 6th floor is so pissed off, he runs down to the ground floor and says, “What the fuck is your problem I said I needed a handsaw!” The other guy says, “I knew that! I was trying to tell you - I'm coming.”

A salesman drove into a small town where a circus was in process. A sign read: “Don't Miss The Amazing Scotsman”. The salesman bought a ticket and sat down. There, on center stage, was a table with three walnuts on it. Standing next to it was an old Scotsman. Suddenly the old man lifted his kilt, whipped out his huge member and smashed all three walnuts with three mighty swings! The crowd erupted in applause as the elderly Scot was carried off on the shoulders of the crowd. Ten years later the salesman visited the same little town and saw the faded sign for the same circus and the same sign “Don't Miss The Amazing Scotsman”. He couldn't believe the old guy was still alive, much less still doing his act! He bought a ticket. Again, the center ring was illuminated. This time, however, instead of walnuts, three coconuts were placed on the table. The Scotsman stood before them, then suddenly lifted his kilt and smashed the coconuts with three swings of his amazing member. The crowd went wild! Flabbergasted, the salesman requested a meeting with him after the show. "You're incredible!" he told the Scotsman. "But I have to know something. You're older now, why switch from walnuts to coconuts?" "Well," said the Scot, "Me eyes are nae whit they used to be!!."

THIS IS WHY GOD INVENTED MENOPAUSE

With all the new technology regarding fertility, a 65-year-old woman gave birth to a baby. When she was discharged from the hospital and went home, her relatives came to visit. "May we see the new baby?" one asked "Not yet," said the 65-year-old mother. Soon, ten minutes had passed and another relative asked, "May we see the new baby now?" "Not yet," said the mother. After another few minutes had elapsed, they asked again, "May we see the baby now?" "No," replied the mother. Growing very impatient, they asked, "Well, when CAN we see the baby?" "When it cries," she told them. "WHEN IT CRIES?" they demanded. "Why do we have to wait until it CRIES?" "Because -- I forgot where I put it."

TRUEISMS

1. If you're too open-minded, your brains will fall out.
2. Don't worry about what people think; they don't do it very often.
3. Going to a church doesn't make you a Christian any more than standing in a garage makes you a car.
4. It isn't the jeans that make your butt look fat.
5. Artificial intelligence is no match for natural stupidity.
6. My idea of housework is to sweep the room with a glance.
7. Not one shred of evidence supports the notion that life is serious.
8. It is easier to get forgiveness than permission.

9. For every action, there is an equal & opposite government program.
10. If you look like your passport picture, you probably need the trip.
11. Bills travel through the mail at twice the speed of checks.
12. A conscience is what hurts when all your other parts feel good.
13. Eat well, stay fit, die anyway. (Just remember how lucky you were to get a free trip around the sun.)
14. Men are from earth. Women are from earth. Deal with it.
15. No man has ever been shot while doing the dishes.
16. A balanced diet is a cookie in each hand.
17. Middle age is when broadness of the mind & narrowness of the waist change places.
18. Opportunities always look bigger going than coming.
19. Junk is something you've kept for years & throw away three weeks before you need it.
20. There is always one more imbecile than you counted on.
21. Experience is a wonderful thing. It enables you to recognize a mistake when you make it again.
22. By the time you can make the ends meet, they move the ends.
23. Thou shall not weigh more than thy refrigerator.
24. Someone who thinks logically provides a nice contrast to the real world.
25. If you must choose between two evils, chose the one that you've never tried before.
26. Never lick a steak knife.
27. Do not attempt to fasten something to the ceiling using a hot glue gun.

Long ago when men cursed and beat the ground with sticks, it was called witchcraft........ Today, it's called golf.

Two guys are moving about in a Wal-Mart when their carts collide.
One says to the other, "Excuse me, but I'm looking for my wife."

What a coincidence, so am I, and I'm getting a little desperate."
"Well, maybe I can help you. What does your wife look like?"
"She's tall, with dark hair, long legs, firm boobs, and a tight ass.
What's your wife look like?" "Never mind, I'll help you look for yours."

Walking through the woods a man comes upon another man hugging a tree with his ear firmly against the tree. Seeing this he inquires, "Just out of curiosity, what the hell are you doing?" "I'm listening to the music of the tree." "You gotta be kiddin me." "No. Would you like to give it a try?" "Well, OK..." So he wraps his arms around the tree and presses his ear up against the tree. With this the other guy slaps a set of hand cuffs on him, takes his wallet, jewelry, car keys, then strips him butt naked and leaves. Two hours later another nature lover strolls by, sees this guy hand cuffed to the tree, stark ass naked and asked, "What the hell happened to you?" He tells the guy the whole story about how he got there, but while he was doing so the guy shakes his head in sympathy walks around behind him, kisses him tenderly behind the ear and says. "Buddy, this just ain't your day."

A lady goes to the bar on a cruise ship and orders a Scotch with two drops of water. As the bartender gives her the drink she says, "I'm on this cruise to celebrate my 80th birthday and it's today."
The bartender says "Well, since it's your birthday, I'll buy you a drink. In fact, this one is on me." As the woman finishes her drink, the woman to her right says, "I would like to buy you a drink, too."
The old woman says, "Thank you. Bartender, I want a Scotch with two drops of water." "Coming up," says the bartender. As she finishes that drink, the man to her left says, "I would like to buy you one, too." The old woman says,

"Thank you." "Bartender, I want another Scotch with two drops of water." "Coming right up," the bartender says. As he gives her the drink he says, "Ma'am, I'm dying of curiosity. Why the Scotch with only two drops of water?" The old woman replies, "Sonny, when you're my age, you've learned how to hold your liquor. Water, however, is a whole other issue."

In a tiny village on the Irish coast lived an old lady, a virgin and very proud of it. Sensing that her final days were rapidly approaching, and desiring to make sure everything was in proper order when she dies, she went to the town's undertaker (who also happened to be the local postal clerk) to make the proper "final" arrangements. As a last wish, she informed the undertaker that she wanted the following inscription engraved on her tombstone: "BORN A VIRGIN, LIVED AS A VIRGIN, DIED A VIRGIN". Not long after, the old maid died peacefully. A few days after the funeral, as the undertaker-- postal clerk went to prepare the tombstone that the lady had requested, it became quite apparent that the tombstone that she had selected was much too small for the wording that she had chosen. He thought long and hard about how he could fulfill the old maid's final request, considering the very limited space available on the small piece of stone. For days, he agonized over the dilemma. But finally his experience as a postal worker allowed him to come up with what he thought was the appropriate solution to the problem. The virgin's tombstone was finally completed and duly engraved, and it read as follows: "RETURNED UNOPENED".

We always hear "the rules" from the female side. Now here are the rules from the male side. These are our rules!

1. Learn to work the toilet seat. You're a big girl. If it's up, put it down. We need it up, you need it down. You don't hear us complaining about you leaving it down.
2. Sunday = sports. It's like the full moon or the changing of the tides. Let it be.

3. Shopping is NOT a sport. And no, we are never going to think of it that way.
4. Crying is blackmail.
5. A headache that lasts for 17 months is a problem. See a doctor.
6. Ask for what you want. Let us be clear on this one: Subtle hints do not work! Strong hints do not work. Obvious hints do not work! Just say it!
7. Yes and No are perfectly acceptable answers to almost every question.
8. Come to us with a problem only if you want help solving it. That's what we do. Sympathy is what your girlfriends are for.
9. Anything we said 6 months ago is inadmissible in an argument. In fact, all comments become null and void after 7 days.
10. If you won't dress like the Victoria's Secret girls, don't expect us to act like soap opera guys.
11. If you think you're fat, you probably are. Don't ask us.
12. If something we said can be interpreted two ways, and one of the ways makes you sad or angry, we meant the other one.
13. You can either ask us to do something or tell us how you want it done. Not both. If you already know best how to do it, just do it yourself.
14. Whenever possible, please say whatever you have to say during commercials.
15. Christopher Columbus did not need directions and neither do we.
16. ALL men see in only 16 colors, like Windows default settings. Peach, for example, is a fruit, not a color. Pumpkin is also a fruit. We have no idea what mauve is.
17. If it itches, it will be scratched. We do that.
18. If we ask what is wrong and you say "nothing," we will act like nothing's wrong. We know you are lying, but it is just not worth the hassle.
19. You have enough clothes.
20. If you ask a question you don't want an answer to, expect

an answer you don't want to hear.

21. When we have to go somewhere, absolutely anything you wear is fine…Really.
22. Don't ask us what we're thinking about unless you are to discuss such topics as baseball, the shotgun formation, or monster trucks.
23. You have too many shoes.
24. I am in shape. Round is a shape.
25. Thank you for reading this; Yes, I know, I have to sleep on the couch tonight, but did you know men really don't mind that, it's like camping.

Eventually you will reach a point when you stop lying about your age and start bragging about it.

The older we get, there are fewer things seem worth waiting in line for.

Some people try to turn back their odometers. Not me, I want people to know "why" I look this way. I've traveled a long way and some of the roads weren't paved.

When you are dissatisfied and would like to go back to youth, think of Calculus and Algebra.

You know you are getting old when everything either dries up or leaks.

One of the many things no one tells you about aging is that it is such a nice change from being young.

One must wait until evening to see just how splendid the day has been. Ah, being young is beautiful, but being old is oh so comfortable.

How old would you be, if you didn't know how old you are?

Old age is when former classmates are so gray and wrinkled and bald, they don't recognize you.

If you don't learn to laugh at trouble while you are young, you won't have anything to laugh at when you are old.

First you forget names, then you forget faces. Then you forget to pull up your zipper, then...Oh my goodness, you forgot to pull your zipper down!

A mechanic was removing a cylinder head from the motor of a Harley when he spotted a well-known heart surgeon in his shop. The surgeon was there waiting for the service manager to come take a look at his bike when the mechanic shouted across the garage, “Hey Doc, can I ask you a question?” The surgeon, a bit surprised, walked over to where the mechanic was working on the motorcycle. The mechanic straightened up, wiped his hands on a rag and asked, “So Doc, look at this engine. I open its heart, take the valves out, repair any damage, and then put them back in, and when I finish, it works just like new. So how come I get such a small salary and you get the really big bucks, when you and I are doing basically the same work?” The surgeon paused, smiled and said to the mechanic, “Try doing it with the engine running”.

<u>Fun Facts</u>

If you farted consistently for 6 years and 9 months, enough gas is produced to create the energy of an atomic bomb.

If you yelled for 8 years, 7 months and 6 days you would have produced enough sound energy to heat one cup of coffee. (Hardly seems worth it.)

A pig's orgasm lasts 30 minutes. (In my next life, I want to be a pig.)

A cockroach will live nine days without its head before it starves to death.

Banging your head against a wall uses 150 calories an hour. (Still thinking about the pig)

The catfish has over 27,000 taste buds. (What could be so tasty on the bottom of a pond?)

Some lions mate over 50 times a day. (I still want to be a pig in my next life)

Right-handed people live, on average, nine years longer than left-handed people. (If you're ambidextrous, do you split the difference?)

A cat's urine glows under a black light. (I wonder who was paid to figure that out?)

Polar bears are left-handed. (If they switch, they'll live a lot longer.)

Humans and dolphins are the only species that have sex for pleasure. (What about that pig??)

On a wall in a ladies room......My husband follows me everywhere. Written just below it........I do not

Q. Why are married women heavier than single women?
A. Single women come home, see what's in the fridge and go to bed. Married women come home see what's in bed and go to the fridge.

He said...I don't now why you wear a bra; you've got nothing to put in it
She said...You wear pants don't you?

He said...Shall we try swapping positions tonight?
She said...That's a good idea -- you stand by the ironing board while I sit on the sofa.

He said…What have you been doing with all the grocery money I gave you?
She said…Turn sideways and look in the mirror!

Q. How many honest, intelligent, caring men in the world does it take to do the dishes?
A. Both of them.

Q. How does a man show that he is planning for the future?
A. He buys two cases of beer.

Q. What is the difference between men and government bonds?
A. The bonds mature.

Q. Why are blonde jokes so short?
A. So men can remember them.

Q. How many men does it take to change a roll of toilet paper?
A. We don't know; it has never happened.

Q. Why is it difficult to find men who are sensitive, caring and good looking?
A. They already have boyfriends.

A three year old boy in his bath examined his testicles and asked, "Mommy, are these my brains?" Mom said, "Not yet, honey."

Q. What do you call a woman who knows where her husband is every night?
A. A widow.

Q. What is the one thing that all men at singles bars have in common?
A. They're married.

Man ask "God, why did you make woman so beautiful?" God says: "So you would love her." "But God," the man says, "why did you make her so dumb?" God says: "So she would love you."

Two men waiting at the pearly gates strike up a conversation. "How'd you die?" the first man asks the second. "I froze to death," says the second. "That's awful. How does it feel to freeze to death?" asks the first guy. "It's very uncomfortable. At first, you get the shakes and you get pains in all your fingers and toes. But eventually, it's a very calm way to go. You get numb and you kind of drift off, as if you're sleeping. How did you die?" asks the second guy. "I had a heart attack" says the first guy. "You see, I knew my wife was cheating on me, so one day I showed up at home unexpectedly. I ran up to the bedroom and found her alone, knitting. I ran down to the basement, but no one was hiding there. I ran up to the second floor, but no one was hiding there either. I ran as fast as I could to the attic, and just as I got there, I had a massive heart attack and died." The second guy shakes his head and says, "That's so ironic." The first guy asks, "What do you mean?" The second guy replies, "If you had only stopped to look in the freezer, we'd both still be alive."

Q. What is the difference between Electrical Engineers and Civil Engineers?

A. Electrical Engineers build weapon systems. Civil Engineers build targets.

DIARIES

HERS

Sunday night - I thought he was acting weird. We had made plans to meet at a bar to have a drink. I was shopping with my friends all day long, so I thought he was upset at the fact that I was a bit late, but he made no comment. Conversation wasn't flowing so I suggested that we go somewhere quiet so we could talk, he agreed but he kept quiet and absent. I asked him what was wrong - he said, "Nothing." I asked him if it was my fault that he was upset. He said it had nothing to do with me and not to worry. On the way home I told him that I loved him, he simply smiled and kept driving. I can't explain his behavior; I don't know why he didn't say, “I love you, too.” When we got home I felt as if I had lost him, as if he wanted nothing to do with me anymore. He just sat there and watched TV; he seemed distant and absent. Finally, I decided to go to bed. About 10 minutes later he came to bed and to my surprise he responded to my caress and we made love, but I still felt that he was distracted and his thoughts were somewhere else. I decided that I could not take it anymore so I decided to confront him with the situation, but he had fallen asleep. I started crying and cried until I, too, fell asleep. I don't know what to do. I'm almost sure that his thoughts are with someone else. My life is a disaster.

HIS
Today the Lions lost, but at least I got laid.

Hussein Family Tree
Now that Uday & Qusay have been eliminated, a lot of the lesser known family members are coming to the attention of American authorities.
Among the brothers...........
Sooflay........................the restaurateur.
Guday. ....the half-Australian brother.
Huray . ...the sports fanatic.
Bejay.. ....the gay brother.
Kuntay & Kintay ....the twins from the African mother.
Sayhay ....the baseball player.
Ojay ... .the stalker / murderer.
Gulay . ...the singer / entertainer.
Ebay ... .the internet czar.
Biliray ....the country music star.
Ecksray ....the radiologist.
Puray.. ....the blender factory owner.
Regay . ...the half-Jamaican brother.
Tupay . ...the one with bad hair.

Among the sisters..............
Pusay..........................the "loose" 22 yr old.
Lattay..........................the coffee shop owner.
Dushay........................the clean sister.
Phayray.......................the zoo worker in the gorilla house.
Sapheway....................the grocery store owner.
Ollay...........................the half-Mexican sister.
Gudlay........................the prostitute.

<u>There are some strange and funny laws still on the books in many states.</u>

New York City

Women may go topless in public, providing it is not being used as a business.

While riding in an elevator, one must talk to no one and fold his hands while looking toward the door.

Citizens may not greet each other by "putting ones thumb to the nose and wiggling the fingers."

Slippers are not to be worn after 10 pm.

It is illegal for a woman to be on the street wearing "body hugging clothing."

Illinois

You may be arrested for vagrancy, if you do not have at least one dollar bill on your person.

Law forbids eating in a place that is on fire.

It is an offence to feed whisky to a dog.

It is illegal for anyone to give lighted cigars to dogs, cats, and other domesticated animals kept as pets.

It is legal to protest naked in front of city hall, as long as you are under 17 years of age and have legal permits.

Oklahoma

Dogs must have a permit signed by the mayor, in order to congregate in groups of three or more on private property.

It is illegal to have the hind legs of farm animals in your boots.

Oral sex is a misdemeanor, and is punishable by one year in jail and a $2,500 fine.

Anyone arrested for soliciting a hooker must have his name and picture shown on television.

Florida

Prohibits topless walking within a 150-foot zone between the beach and the street.

It is considered an offence to shower naked.

You may not kiss your wife's breasts.

In Sarasota, if you hit a pedestrian you are fined $78.

It is illegal to jog with your eyes closed.

Phoenix, Arizona - Every man who enters the city limits must wear pants.

Willowdale, Oregon - No man may curse while having sex with his wife.

And...In some parts of the South, a widow or divorced

woman isn't allowed to dry her underwear on the front porch or on a clothesline before the sun goes down.

A husband read an article to his wife about how many words women use a day 30,000 to a man's 15,000. The wife replied, “The reason has to be because we have to repeat everything to men”. The husband then turned to his wife and asked, “What?”

While attending a Marriage Seminar dealing with communication, Tom and his wife Grace listened to the instructor, “It is essential that husbands and wives know the things that are important to each other.” He addressed a man, “Can you describe your wife's favorite flower?” Tom leaned over, touched his wife's arm gently and whispered, “It's Pillsbury, isn't it?”

A couple drove down a country road for several miles, not saying a word. An earlier discussion had led to an argument and neither of them wanted to concede their position. As they passed a barnyard of mules, goats, and pigs, the husband asked sarcastically, “Relatives of yours?” “Yep,” the wife replied, “in-laws.”

Men are like...........
Laxatives....................They irritate the shit out of you.
Bananas......................The older they get, the less firm they are.
Vacations ....They never seem to be long enough.
The weather ....Nothing can be done to change them.
Blenders.....................You need one, but you're not quite sure why.
Chocolate Bars...........Sweet, smooth, and they usually head right for your hips.
Commercials..............You can't believe a word they say.
Department stores......Their clothes are always ½ off.
Government bonds.....They take so long to mature.

Popcorn .... They satisfy you, but only for a little while.
Mascara .... They usually run at the first sign of emotion.
Snowstorms .... You never know when they're coming, how many inches you'll get or how long it'll last
Parking Spots .... All the good ones are taken, the rest are handicapped.
Lava Lamps .... Fun to look at, but not very bright.

Military Truisms

A slipping gear could let your M203 grenade launcher fire when you least expect it. That would make you quite unpopular in what's left of your unit. (Army's magazine of preventive maintenance).

Aim towards the Enemy. (Instruction printed on US Rocket Launcher).

When the pin is pulled, Mr. Grenade is not our friend. (US Marine Corps)

Cluster bombing from B-52s is very, very accurate. The bombs always hit the ground. (US Air Force)

If the enemy is in range, so are you. (Infantry Journal)

It is generally inadvisable to eject directly over the area you just bombed. (US Air Force Manual)

Whoever said the pen is mightier than the sword obviously never encountered automatic weapons. (Gen MacArthur)

Try to look unimportant; they may be low on ammo. (Infantry Journal)

Tracers work both ways. (US Army Ordnance)

Five-second fuses only last three seconds. (Infantry Journal)

Any ship can be a minesweeper... once. (Admiral Hornblower)

Don't ever be the first, don't ever be the last, and don't ever volunteer to do anything. (US Navy Swabbie)

Bravery is being the only one who knows you're afraid. (David Hackworth)

If your attack is going too well, you have walked into an ambush. (Infantry Journal)

No combat-ready unit has ever passed inspection. No inspection-ready unit ever survived combat (Joe Gay)

Never tell the Platoon Sergeant you have nothing to do. (Unknown Marine Recruit)

Don't draw fire; it irritates the people around you. (Your Buddies)

Mines are equal-opportunity weapons. (Saddam Hussein)

On some air bases the Air Force is on one side of the field and civilian aircraft use the other side of the field, with the control tower in the middle. One day the tower received a call from an aircraft asking, “What time is it?” The tower responded, “Who is calling?” The aircraft replied, “What difference does it make?” The tower replied “It makes a lot of difference. If it is an American Airlines flight, it is 3 o'clock. If it is an Air Force plane, it is 1500 hours. If it is a Navy aircraft, it is 6 bells. If it is an Army aircraft, the big hand is on the 12 and the little hand is on the 3. If it is a Marine Corps aircraft, it's Thursday afternoon and 120 minutes to “Happy Hour.”

Q: How do you know if there is a fighter pilot at your party?
A: He'll tell you.

During training exercises, the lieutenant who was driving down a muddy back road encountered another car stuck in the mud with a red-faced colonel at the wheel. “Your jeep stuck, sir?” asked the lieutenant as he pulled alongside. “Nope,” replied the colonel, coming over and handing him the keys, “Yours is.”

Officer: “Soldier, do you have change for a dollar?”
Soldier: “Sure, buddy.”
Officer: “That's no way to address an officer! Now let's try it again!”
Officer: “Soldier. Do you have change for a dollar?”
Soldier: “No, SIR!”

Having just moved into his new office, a pompous, new colonel was sitting at his desk when an airman knocked on the door. Conscious of his new position, the colonel quickly picked up the phone, told the airman to enter then said into the phone, “Yes, General, I'll be seeing him this afternoon and I'll pass along your message. In the meantime, thank you for your good wishes, sir.” Feeling as though he had sufficiently impressed the young enlisted man, he asked, “What do you want?” “Nothing important, sir,” the airman replied, “I'm just here to hook up your telephone.”

Q: What's the difference between God and fighter pilots
A: God doesn't think he's a fighter pilot.

Q: What's the difference between a fighter pilot and a jet engine?
A: A jet engine stops whining when the plane shuts down.

An Air Force Chief Master Sergeant and a General were sitting in the barbershop. They were both just getting finished with their shaves, when the barbers reached for some after-shave to slap on their faces. The General shouted, “Hey, don't put that stuff on me! My wife will think I've been in a whorehouse!” The Chief turned to his barber and said, “Go ahead and put it on. My wife doesn't know what the inside of a whorehouse smells like.”

“Well,” snarled the tough old Navy Chief to the bewildered Seaman. “I suppose after you get discharged from the Navy, you'll just be waiting for me to die so you can come and piss on my grave.” “Not me, Chief!” the Seaman replied. “Once I get out of the Navy, I'm never going to stand in line again!”

A big earthquake with the strength of 8.1 on the Richter scale has hit Mexico. Two million Mexicans have died and over a million are injured. The country is totally ruined and the government doesn't know where to start with providing help to rebuild. The rest of the world is in shock. Canada is sending troopers to help the Mexican army control the riots. The European community (except France) is sending food and money. The United States, not to be outdone, is sending two million replacement Mexicans.

A couple orders the “Chicken Surprise” at a Chinese restaurant. The waiter brings the meal, served in a lidded pot. Just as the wife is about to serve herself, the lid rises slightly. Two little eyes look around before the lid slams back down. “Good grief, did you see that?” she asks her husband. He didn't, so she asks him to look in the pot. Again, the lid rises. He sees two little eyes before it slams down. He calls the waiter over and demands an explanation. “I made a mistake,” says the waiter. “I brought you Peeking Duck.”

A Polish man married a Canadian woman after he had been in Canada a year or so. Although his English was far from perfect, they got on very well until one day he rushed into a lawyer's office and asked him if he could arrange a divorce for him “very quick”. The lawyer said that the speed of

getting a divorce would depend on the circumstances and asked him the following questions:
Lawyer: “Have you any grounds?”
Pole: “JA, JA, an acre and half and a nice little home with 3 bedrooms.”
Lawyer “No, I mean what is the foundation of this case?”
Pole: “It is made of concrete, brick and mortar,” he responded.
Lawyer: “Does either of you have a real grudge?”
Pole: “No,” he replied, “We have a two-car carport and have never really needed one.”
Lawyer: “I mean, What are your relations like?”
Pole: “All my relations are in Poland.”
Lawyer: “Is there any infidelity in your marriage?”
Pole: “Yes, we have hi fidelity stereo set & DVD player with 6.1 sound. We don't necessarily like the music, but the answer to your questions is yes.”
Lawyer: “No, I mean does your wife beat you up?”
Pole: “NO, I'm always up before her.”
Lawyer: “Is your wife a nagger?”
Pole: “NO, she white.”
Lawyer: “Why do you want this divorce?”
Pole: “She going to kill me.”
Lawyer: “What makes you think that?”
Pole: “I got proof.”
Lawyer: “What kind of proof?”
Pole: “She going to poison me. She buy a bottle at the drug store and put on shelf in bathroom. I can read it says Polish Remover.”

A young man tells his mother he's fallen in love and that he is going to get married. He says, “Just for fun, Mom, I'm going to bring over 3 women and you try and guess which one I'm going to marry.” The mother agrees. The next day, he brings three beautiful women into the house and sits them down on the couch and they chat for a while. He then says, “Okay, Mom, guess which one I'm going to marry.” She immediately replies, “The one on the right.” That's amazing,

Mom. You're right. How did you know?" The mother replies "I don't like her."

A woman walks into the downtown welfare office, trailed by 15 kids... "WOW," the social worker exclaims, "Are they ALL YOURS???" "Yes' am they is all mine," the flustered momma sighs, having heard that question a thousand times before. She says, "Sit down Leroy." All the children rush to find seats. "Well," says the social worker, "then you must be here to sign up. I'll need all your children's names." "This one's my oldest, his name is Leroy." "OK, and who's next?" "Well, this one, he is Leroy also." The social worker raises an eyebrow but continues. One by one, through the oldest four, all boys, all named Leroy. Then she is introduced to the eldest girl, named Leighroy! "All right...," says the caseworker, "I'm seeing a pattern here...Are they ALL named Leroy?" Their Mamma replied, "Well, yes it makes it easier. When its time to get them out of bed and ready for school, I just yells, 'Leroy!' An' when it's time for dinner, I just yell 'Leroy!' an' they all comes a runnin. An' if I need to stop the kid who's running into the street, I just yell 'Leroy' and all of them stop. It's the smartest idea I ever had, namin' them all Leroy." The social worker thinks this over for a bit, then wrinkles her forehead and says tentatively, "But what if you just want ONE kid to come, and not the whole bunch?" "Ah, that's so easy," said the momma. "Then I calls them by their last names"

The Lord came to Noah, in Canada, in the year 2001. The earth was wicked and over-populated. The Lord instructed Noah to build another Ark and save two of every living thing along with a few good humans. "Here's the blueprint" said the Lord. "Hurry, in six months I start the unending rain for 40 days and 40 nights." Six months later the rain started. The Lord looked down and saw Noah weeping in his flooded yard and no ark. "Noah" He roared, "Where is the Ark?" "Forgive me, Lord," begged Noah. "Things have changed. I needed a building permit. I've been arguing with the inspector about the need for a sprinkler system. My neighbors claim that I have violated the neighborhood zoning laws by building the Ark in my yard and the height limitation being exceeded. We had to go to the Development Appeal Board for a decision. Then Transport Canada and the Department of Highways and Hydro wanted a bond posted for the future costs of moving power, trolley and other overhead obstructions, to clear the passage for the Ark's move to the sea. I argued the sea would be coming to us, but they would hear nothing of this. Getting the wood was another problem. There's a ban on cutting local trees in order to save the spotted owl. I tried to convince environmentalists that I needed the wood to save the owls. No go! I gathered the animals, but then I got sued by an animal rights group. They insisted that I was confining wild animals against their will. As well, they argued the accommodation was too restrictive and it was cruel and inhumane to put so many animals in so confined a space. Environment Canada decided that I could not build the Ark without filing an environmental impact statement on your proposed flood. I'm still trying to resolve a complaint with the Human Rights Commission on how many minorities I'm supposed to hire for my building crew. The trades union wants me to hire only Union trades-people with Ark building experience. To make matters worse, Canada Customs and Revenue Agency seized all my assets, claiming I'm trying to leave the country illegally as well as with endangered species. So, forgive me, Lord, but it would take at least ten years to finish this Ark." Suddenly the skies cleared and the sun began to shine. A rainbow stretched across the sky. Noah looked up in wonder. "You mean you're not going to destroy the world?" he asked. "No", said the Lord. "The Government beat me to it"

A lot of folks can't understand how we came to have an oil shortage here in our country. Well, there's a very simple answer. Nobody bothered to check the oil. We just didn't know we were getting low. The reason for that is purely geographical. Our OIL is located in Alaska, California, Coastal Florida, Coastal Louisiana, Kansas, Oklahoma, Pennsylvania and Texas but our all the DIPSTICKS are located in Washington DC. Any Questions

Bob, a 65-year old "Old Fart" went for his annual physical. All of his tests came back with normal results. Doctor Lund said, "Bob, everything looks great physically. How are you doing mentally and emotionally? Are you at peace with yourself and do you have a good relationship with God?" Bob replied, "God and me are really tight. He knows I have poor eyesight, so he's fixed it so that when I get up in the middle of the night to go to the bathroom "poof" the light goes on, when I'm done "poof" the light goes off." "Wow!" commented Dr. Lund, "That's incredible!" A little later in the day Dr. Lund called Bob's wife. "Paula, Bob is doing fine. Physically he's great. But, I had to call because I'm in awe of his relationship with God. Is it true that he gets up during the night and "poof" the light goes on in the bathroom and then when he is through "poof" the light goes off?" Paula exclaimed, "Oh, my God! He's peeing in the refrigerator again!"

A family is at the dinner table. The son asks his father, "Dad, how many kinds of boobies are there?" The father, surprised, answers, "Well, son, there's three kinds of breasts. In her twenties, women's breasts are like melons, round and firm. In her thirties to forties, they are like pears, still nice but hanging a bit. After fifty, they are like onions." "Onions?" "Yes, you see them and they make you cry." This infuriated his wife and daughter so the daughter said, "Mum, how many kinds of 'willies' are there?" The mother who is surprised, smiles and answers, Well dear, a man goes through three phases. In his twenties, his 'willie' is like an oak tree, mighty and hard. In his thirties and forties, it is a birch, flexible but reliable. After his fifties, it is like a Christmas tree." "A Christmas tree?" "Yes, dead from the root up and the balls are for decoration only."

Joe was a successful lawyer but he was increasingly hampered by incredible headaches. When his career and love life started to suffer, he sought medical help. After being referred from one specialist to another, he finally came across an old country doctor who solved the problem. “The good news is that I can cure your headaches. The bad news is that it will require castration. You have a very rare condition, which causes your testicles to press up against the base of your spine and the pressure creates a terrible headache. The only way to relieve the condition is to remove your testicles.” Joe was shocked and depressed. He wondered whether he had anything to live for. He couldn't even concentrate long enough to answer his own question, but decided he had no choice but to go under the knife. When he left the hospital after the surgery he was without a headache for the first time in 20 years, but he also felt like he was missing an important part of himself. As he walked down the street he realized that he felt like a different person. He could make a new beginning and live a new life. He saw a men's clothing store and thought, “That's what I need, a new suit.” He entered the shop and told the salesman, “I'd like a new suit”, and picked one out. The elderly tailor eyed him briefly and said, “Let's see....size 44 long.” Joe laughed, “That's right, how did you know?” “Been in the business 60 years.” he replied. Joe tried on the suit and it fit him perfectly. As Joe admired himself, the salesman said, “How about a new shirt?” Joe thought for a moment then said, “Sure.” The salesman eyed Joe, and said, “34” sleeve and a 16” neck?” Joe was surprised. “That's right, how did you know?” “Been in the business 60 years.” said the tailor. Joe tried on the shirt, and it fitted perfectly. As Joe adjusted the collar in the mirror, the salesman said, “How about new shoes?” Joe was on a roll and said, “Sure.” The salesman eyed Joe's feet and said, “Let's see...9?” Joe was astonished, “How did you know?” “Been in the business 60 years.” Joe tried on the shoes and they fit perfectly. He walked comfortably around the shop and the salesman said, “How about some new underwear?" Joe thought for a second and said, "Sure." The salesman stepped back, eyed Joe's waist and said, "Let's see...size 36." Joe laughed, "Ah ha! I got you! I've worn size 34 since I was 18 years old.." The salesman shook his head, "You can't wear size 34. A 34 would press your testicles up against your spine giving you one hell of a headache."

Two Pollock men are out hunting in the Molokai forests when one of them falls to the ground. He doesn't seem to be breathing, and his eyes are rolled back in his head. The other guy whips out his cell phone and calls 911. He gasps to the operator, "I think my friend is dead, what should I do? The operator, hoping to calm the caller, says in a relaxed tone "Just take it easy, I can help. First lets make sure he's dead" There is silence, then a shot is heard. The Pollock says, "OK, now what?"

Two Pollock builders were working on a house. One Pollock was on a ladder nailing. He'd reach into his nail pouch, pull out a nail, look at it, and either toss it over his shoulder or proceed to nail it into the wood. The other Pollock couldn't stand it any longer and yelled up, "Why are you throwing some of the nails away?" The first Pollock explained, "When I pull it out of my nail pouch, if it's pointed toward me I throw it away. If it's pointed toward the house, then I can use it!" The second Pollock explained "Idiot, don't throw away those nails that are pointed toward you! They're for the other side of the house!!"

A Redneck, a Chinese, and a Pollock, all first time fathers, are pacing nervously in the maternity ward waiting room when a nurse rushes out of the delivery room holding a black baby. "Is it yours?" she asks the Redneck. "Certainly not," he retorts. "Yours?" she asks the Chinese, who vigorously denies paternity. "How about you?" she asks the Pollock. "Maybe," he says glumly. "My wife burns everything."

There was a Cracker, an Asian, and a Pollock on death row.

The warden gave them a choice of three ways to die: Be shot, be hung or be injected with the A.I.D.S. virus. So the Cracker said, “Shoot me right in the head.” (Bang, he was dead). Then the Asian said, “Just hang me.”(Snap, he was dead). Then the Pollock said, “Give me some of that AIDS stuff.” They gave him the shot, and the Pollock fell down laughing. The guards looked at each other and wondered what was wrong with this guy. Then the Pollock said, “Give me another one of those shots”, so the guards did. Now the Pollock was laughing so hard, tears rolled from his eyes and he doubled over. So finally the warden said, “What the hell is wrong with you?” The Pollock replied, “You guys are sooo stupid .....I’m wearing a condom.”

I went to the store the other day, and I was only in there about 5 minutes when I came out and there was a city cop writing out a parking ticket. I went up to him and said, “Come on buddy, how about giving a senior a break?” He ignored me and continued writing the ticket. I called him a name. He glared at me and started writing another ticket for having worn tires. So I called him a worse name. He finished writing the second ticket and put it on the windshield with the first. This went on for about 20 minutes. The more I abused him, the more tickets he wrote. I didn't care, my car was parked around the corner.

This pre-booty call agreement (hereinafter referred to as the “Agreement”) is entered into on the _____ day of __________, 2002, by________________________, between _____________and______________.

THIS AGREEMENT SHALL COVER THE FOLLOWING RULES AND PRINCIPLES:

1. No sleeping over unless it is very good and we need to repeat it in the morning.
2. No meeting in public except for dinner or drinks before the events of the evening.
3. No calls before 9 PM we don't have shit to talk about.

4. None of that “lovemaking” shit - only sex allowed.
5. No emotional discussions (i.e. Where are we heading with this? Do you love me?) The answer is no, so don't ask.
6. No plans made in advance - that is why you are called the “backup,” unless you are from out-of-town, then it's only a one time advanced arrangement.
7. All gifts accepted - money is always good.
8. No asking for comparisons with former lovers, it's really none of your damn business.
9. No baby talk, however, dirty talk is encouraged.
10. No calling each other “friends with privileges” we are not friends, just sex buddies.
11. Calling out the wrong name during sex is OK don't be offended.
12. No extra clothing I don't want your ass leaving anything behind when you leave.
13. No falling asleep right after sex, it's over, so get your ass up, get dressed and go the fuck home.
14. Don't be offended if I don't ask if you enjoyed it - I don't care.
15. You cannot borrow my car for any reason.
16. No condoms, no fucking. Carry your ass home.
17. Doggie style is the preferred position, the less eye contact the better.
18. If anyone asks who you are, the standard response will be: “My roommate's girlfriend/boyfriend.”
19. Bring your own drink - I am not your liquor store.
20. No phone use, please - don't want anyone calling back looking for your ass.

* EXTRA TIP FOR SUCCESSFUL BOOTY CALLS:
The aforementioned rules may only be altered by the holder of the agreement. If the other party attempts to change or alter any terms of this Agreement, it will automatically become null and void and you will then be removed from the BOOTY CALL LIST and deleted from phone memory and email list. In other words, you will be BLOCKED from all communications until your silly ass understands the rules.

Participating Parties

Signature___________________________________
Date:_______________
Signature___________________________________
Date: _______________

The U S Postal Service created a stamp with a picture of Senator Hillary Clinton to honor her achievements as the First Lady of our nation. In daily use it was shown that the stamp was not sticking to envelopes. This enraged Senator Clinton, who demanded a full investigation. After a month of testing, a special presidential commission made the following findings:

1. The stamp was in perfect order.
2. There was nothing wrong with the applied adhesive.
3. People were spitting on the wrong side.

A good-ole-redneck boy staggered home after another late evening with his drinking buddies. With his shoes in hand to avoid waking his wife, he tiptoed as quietly as he could toward the stairs leading to their upstairs bedroom, but misjudged the bottom step in the darkened entry way. As he caught himself by grabbing the banister, his body swung around and he landed heavily on his rump. A whiskey bottle in each back pocket broke and made the landing especially painful. Managing to suppress a yelp, he sprung up, pulled down his pants and examined his lacerated and bleeding cheeks in the mirror of a nearby darkened hallway, then managed to find a large full box of band aids before proceeding to place a patch as best he could on each place he saw blood. After hiding the now almost empty box, he managed to shuffle and stumble his way to bed. In the morning, he awakens with screaming pain in head and butt to find his wife staring at him from across the room, and hears her say: “You were drunk again last night!” Forcing himself to ignore his agony, he looked meekly at her and replied

"Now Honey, why would you say such a mean thing?" "Well," she said, "there is the front door left open, the broken whiskey bottle glass at the bottom of the stairs, the drops of blood trailing through the house, your bloodshot eyes, and all that blood in the bed, but, mostly.... it's all those band aids stuck on the mirror downstairs."

A letter to the American Voter:
During the Clinton Administration I had an extremely good and well paying job. I took numerous vacations and had vacation homes. Since President Bush took office, I have watched my entire life change for the worse. I lost my job, lost my two sons in that terrible Iraqi War, lost my home and lost my health insurance. As a matter of fact, I lost everything and became homeless. Adding insult to injury, when the authorities found me living like an animal, instead of helping me, they arrested me. I will do anything to insure the defeat of the Republicans in the next election. I will do anything to insure that a Democrat is back in the White House come next year. Republicans have to go. I just thought you would like to know how one senior citizen views the Republican Administration. Thank you for taking the time to read my letter.

Sincerely,
(The late) Saddam Hussein

A preacher goes to a nursing home to meet an elderly parishioner. As he is sitting there he notices this bowl of peanuts beside her bed and takes one. As they talk, he can't help himself and eats one after another. By the time they are through talking, the bowl is empty. He says, "Ma'am, I'm so sorry, but I seem to have eaten all of your peanuts." "That's okay," she says. "They would have just sat there. Without my teeth, all I can do is suck the chocolate off and put 'em back in the bowl."

A deserter GI was running down a road escaping from two MPs. He came to a fork in the road and saw a nun standing there. He asked her “Please Sister, may I hide under your skirt for a few minutes. I'll explain why later.” The nun agreed to his request. Shortly thereafter, the two MPs came running along and asked her if she had seen a soldier running down the road. She replied, “He went that way.” After the MPs disappeared, the soldier crawled out from under her skirt and said “I can't thank you enough Sister, but you see I don't want to go to Iraq.” The nun said she understood. The GI said, “I hope you don't think me rude or impertinent, but you have the most beautiful pair of legs I've ever seen!” The nun replied, “If you had looked a little higher, you would have seen the most beautiful pair of balls you've ever seen! I don't want to go to Iraq either!”

BREAKING NEWS........At New York's Kennedy Airport today, an individual later discovered to be a public school teacher was arrested trying to board a flight while in possession of a ruler, a protractor, and a calculator. Authorities believe he is a member of the notorious al-Gebra movement. He is being charged with carrying weapons of math instruction!

One day God was looking down at Earth and saw all of the rascally behavior that was going on. So he called one of His angels and sent the angel to Earth for a time. When he returned, he told God, “Yes, it is bad on Earth; 95% are misbehaving; only 5% are not.” God thought for a moment and said, “Maybe I had better send down a second angel to get another opinion.” So God called another angel and sent him to Earth for a time too. When the angel returned he went to God and said “Yes, it's true. The Earth is in decline; 95% are misbehaving, but 5% are being good.” God was not pleased. So He decided to e-mail the 5% who were being good, because He wanted to encourage them...give them a little something to help them keep going. Do you know what the e-mail said? Okay, just wondering; I didn't get one either...

In 1964, a US Navy cruiser put into port in Mobile, Alabama for a week's R&R. The first evening, the Captain was surprised to receive the following letter from the wife of a very wealthy plantation owner and industrialist:

Dear Captain:
Thursday will be my daughter Susan's debutante ball. I would like you to send four well-mannered, handsome, unmarried officers. They should arrive at 8 p.m. sharp, prepared for an evening of polite Southern conversation and dancing with lovely young ladies. PS: No Jews.

Sure enough, at 8 p.m. on Thursday, the lady followed her butler to answer a rap at the door which was opened by the butler. She found, in dress uniform, four very handsome, exquisitely mannered and smiling African-American naval officers. Her lower jaw hit the floor, but pulling herself together she stammered, "There must be some mistake." "Madam," said the first officer, "Captain Goldberg doesn't make mistakes."

Proudly showing off his new apartment to a couple of his friends late one night, the drunk led the way to his bedroom where there was a big brass gong. "What's that big brass gong?" one of the guests asked. "It's not a gong. It's a talking clock," the drunk replied. "A talking clock? Seriously?" asked his astonished friend. "Yup," replied the drunk. "How's it work?" the 2nd guest asked, squinting at it. "Watch," the drunk replied. He picked up a hammer, gave it an ear shattering pound and stepped back. The three stood looking at one another for a moment. Suddenly, someone on the other side of the wall screamed: "HEY YOU ASSHOLE it's ten past three in the morning!"

Hillary Clinton died and went to heaven. As she stood in front of St. Peter at the Pearly Gates, she saw a huge wall of clocks behind him. She asked, "What are all those clocks?" St. Peter answered, "Those are Lie Clocks. Everyone on

Earth has a Lie Clock. Every time you lie, the hands on your clock will move." "Oh," said Hillary, "Whose clock is that?" "That's Mother Teresa's. The hands have never moved, indicating that she never told a lie." "Whose clock is that?" asked Hillary, pointing to another one. "That's Abraham Lincoln's clock. The hands have only moved twice, telling us that Honest Abe only told 2 lies in his entire life." This fascinates Hillary to no end, so she asks "Where is Bill's clock? He was a famous person!" St. Peter replies, "Bill's clock is in Jesus' office. He's using it as a ceiling fan."

An atheist was taking a walk through the woods. "What majestic trees! What powerful rivers! What beautiful animals!" he said to himself. As he was walking alongside the river, he heard a rustling in the bushes behind him. He turned to look and saw a 7 foot grizzly charge towards him. He ran as fast as he could up the path. He looked over his shoulder and saw that the bear was closing in on him. He looked over his shoulder again, and the bear was even closer. He tripped and fell on the ground. He rolled over to pick himself up but saw the bear right on top of him, reaching for him with his left paw and raising his right paw to strike him. At that instant the Atheist cried out "Oh my God!" Time stopped. The bear froze. The forest was silent. As a bright light shone upon the man, a voice came out of the sky "You deny my existence for all of these years, teach others I don't exist, and even credit creation to a cosmic accident. Do you expect me to help you out of this predicament? Am I to count you as a believer?" The atheist looked directly into the light, "It would be hypocritical of me to suddenly ask you to treat me as a Christian now, but perhaps could you make the BEAR a Christian?" "Very well," said the voice. The light went out. The sounds of the forest resumed. Then the bear dropped his right paw, brought both paws together and bowed his head and spoke "Lord, bless this food which I am about to receive, from thy bounty, through Christ our Lord, Amen."

A very attractive lady goes up to the bar. She gestures alluringly to the bartender who comes over immediately. When he arrives, she seductively signals that he should bring his face closer to hers. When he does, she begins to gently caress his full beard. “Are you the manager?” she asks, softly stroking his face with both hands. “Actually, I'm not,” says the man. “Can you get him for me? I need to speak to him,” she says, running her hands beyond his beard and into his hair. “I'm afraid I can't,” breathes the bartender. “Is there anything I can do?” “Yes there is. I need you to give him a message” she continues, running her forefinger across the bartender's lips and slyly popping a couple of her fingers into his mouth and allowing him to nip them gently. “What should I tell him?” the bartender manages to say around her delicate fingers. “Tell him” she whispers, “there is no toilet paper, hand soap or paper towels in the ladies room.”

An old farmer owned a large farm and had a large pond in the back forty. It was fixed up for swimming, complete with a small sandy beach and picnic tables. One evening the old farmer decided to go down to the pond for a swim. As he neared the pond, he heard women's voices shouting and laughing with glee. As he came closer he saw a bunch of young women skinny-dipping in his pond. They saw him approach and they all went to the deep end of the pond. One of the young women shouted to him “Go away, we're not coming out until you leave!” The old man replied “I didn't come down here to watch you ladies swim or make you get out of the pond, I only came to feed my alligators.”

The teacher gave her fifth grade class an assignment: Get their parents to tell them a story with a moral at the end of it. The next day the kids came back and one by one began to tell their stories. “Johnny, do you have a story to share?” “Yes, ma'am, my daddy told a story about my Aunt Susan. Aunt Susan was a pilot in Desert Storm and her plane got hit. She had to bail out over enemy territory and all she had was a small flask of whiskey, a pistol and a survival knife. She drank the whiskey on the way down so it wouldn't fall into enemy hands and then her parachute landed right in the middle of twenty enemy troops. She shot fifteen of them with the gun until she ran out of bullets, killed four more with the knife, 'til the blade broke and then she killed the last one with her bare hands." "Good heavens," said the horrified teacher, "What kind of moral did your daddy teach you from that horrible story?" "Stay the hell away from Aunt Susan when she's been drinking."

In Jerusalem, an American female journalist heard about an old rabbi who visited the Wailing Wall to pray, twice a day, everyday, for a long, long time. In an effort to check out the story, she goes to the holy site and there he is. She watches the bearded old man at prayer and after about 45 minutes when he turns to leave, she approaches him for an interview. "I'm Rebecca Smith from CNN, sir, how long have you been coming to the Wailing Wall and praying?" "For about 50 years" he informs her. "50 years! That's amazing! What do you pray for?" "I pray for peace between the Jews and the Arabs. I pray for all the hatred to stop and I pray for all our children to grow up in safety and friendship." "And how do you feel, sir, after doing this for 50 years?" "Like I'm talking to a fucking wall."

<u>You know you're a redneck if…</u>

1. You take your dog for a walk and you both use the same tree.
2. You can entertain yourself for more than an hour with a fly swatter.
3. Your property has been mistaken for a recycling center.
4. Your boat has not left the driveway in 15 years.
5. You burn your yard rather than mow it.
6. You think the Nutcracker is something you do off the high dive.
7. The Salvation Army declines your mattress.
8. You think fast food is hitting a deer at 65 mph.
9. You offer to give someone the shirt off your back and they don't want it.

10. You come back from the dump with more than you took.
11. You keep a can of Raid on the kitchen table.
12. Your grandmother has "Ammo" on her Christmas list.
13. You think a subdivision is part of a math problem.
14. You've bathed with flea and tick soap.
15. You know how many bales of hay your car will hold.
16. You have used a rag for a gas cap.
17. Your house doesn't have curtains but your truck does.
18. You wonder how service stations keep their restrooms so clean.
19. You consider your license plate personalized because your father made it.
20. Your lifetime goal is to own a fireworks stand.
21. You have a complete set of salad bowls, and they all say Cool Whip on the side.
22. You've used your ironing board as a buffet table.
23. You think a quarter horse is that ride in front of K-Mart.
24. Your neighbors think you're a detective because a cop always brings you home.
25. You've used a toilet brush as a back scratchier.
26. You missed 5th grade graduation because you had jury duty.

An ambitious corporate yuppie finally decided to take a vacation. He booked himself on a Caribbean cruise and proceeded to have the time of his life... until the boat sank. The man found himself swept up on the shore of an island with no other people, no supplies. Nothing. Only bananas and coconuts. After about four months, he is lying on the beach when one day the most gorgeous woman he has ever seen rows up to him. In disbelief, he asks her, "Where did you come from? How did you get here?" "I rowed from the other side of the island," she said. "I landed here when my cruise ship sank." "Amazing," he said. "You were really lucky to have a rowboat wash up with you." "Oh, this?" replied the woman. "I made the rowboat out of raw material I found on the island; the oars were whittled from gum tree branches; I wove the bottom from palm branches; and the sides and stern came from a Eucalyptus tree."

"But, but, that's impossible," stuttered the man. "You had no tools to make the boat. How did you manage?" "Oh, that was no problem," replied the woman. "On the south side of the island, there is a very unusual strata of alluvial rock exposed. I found if I fired it to a certain temperature in my kiln, it melted into forgeable ductile iron. I used that for tools and used the tools to make the boat". The guy was stunned. "Let's row round to my place, "she said. After a few minutes of rowing, she docks the boat at a small wharf. As the man looks onto shore, he nearly falls out of the boat. Before him is a stone walk leading to an exquisite bungalow painted in blue and white. While the woman ties up the rowboat with an expertly woven hemp rope, the man can only stare ahead, dumbstruck. As they walk into the house, she said casually, "It's not much, but I call it home. Sit down please. Would you like to have a drink?" "No thank you," he said, still dazed. "I can't take anymore coconut juice." "It's not coconut juice," the woman replies. "I have a still. How about a Pina Colada?" Trying to hide his continued amazement, the man accepts, and they sit down on her couch to talk. After they have exchanged their stories, the woman announces, "I'm going to slip into something more comfortable. Would you like to take a shower and shave? There is a razor upstairs in the bathroom cabinet." No longer questioning anything, the man goes into the bathroom. There, in the cabinet, is a razor made from a bone handle. Two shells honed to a hollow ground edge are fastened on to its end inside of a swivel mechanism. "This woman is amazing," he mused. "What next?" When he returns, she greets him wearing nothing but vines, strategically positioned, and smelling faintly of gardenias. She beckons for him to sit down next to her. "Tell me," she began, suggestively, slithering closer to him "We've been out here for a really long time. You've been lonely. There's something I'm sure you really feel like doing right now, something you've been longing to do for all these months?" "I think you know what I'm talking about" she said staring longingly into his eyes. He can't believe what he's hearing: "What - ...?" he swallows excitedly, "you mean ...I can CHECK MY E-MAIL from here?!"

A popular bar had a new robotic bartender installed. A fellow came in for a drink and the robot asked him, “What's your IQ?” The man replied, “130.” So the robot proceeded to make conversation about physics, astronomy, investments, insurance, and so on. The man listened intently and thought, “This is really cool.” Another gent came in for a drink and the robot asked him, “What's your IQ?” The man responded, “100.” So the robot started talking about football, baseball, and so on. The man thought to himself, “Wow, this is really cool.” A third guy came in to the bar. As with the others, the robot asked him, “What's your IQ?” The man replied, “70.” The robot then said, “So, are you Democrats really going to nominate John Kerry?”

<u>LIFE BEFORE THE COMPUTER</u>

1. An application was for employment.
2. A program was a TV show.
3. A cursor used profanity.
4. A keyboard was a piano!
5. Memory was something that you lost with age.
6. A CD was a bank account.
7. And if you had a 3 1/2 inch floppy you hoped nobody found out!
8. Compress was something you did to garbage not something you did to a file.
9. And if you unzipped anything in public you'd be in jail for a while!
10. Log on was adding wood to a fire.
11. Hard drive was a long trip on the road.
12. A mouse pad was where a mouse lived.
13. And a backup happened to your commode!
14. Cut - you did with a pocket knife.
15. Paste you did with glue.
16. A web was a spider's home.
17. And a virus was the flue!

I hear nobody's been killed in a computer crash but when it happens they wish they were dead!!

Two engineering students were walking across campus when one said, “Where did you get such a great bike?” The second engineer replied, “Well, I was walking along yesterday minding my own business when a beautiful woman rode up on this bike. She threw the bike to the ground, took off all her clothes and said “Take what you want.” The second engineer nodded approvingly “Good choice, the clothes probably wouldn't have fit.”

An architect, an artist and an engineer were discussing whether it was better to spend time with the wife or a mistress. The architect said he enjoyed time with his wife, building a solid foundation for an enduring relationship. The artist said he enjoyed time with his mistress, because of the passion and mystery he found there. The engineer said, “I like both.” “Both?” Engineer: “Yeah. If you have a wife and a mistress, they will each assume you are spending time with the other woman, and you can go to the office and get some work done.”

To the optimist, the glass is half full.
To the pessimist, the glass is half empty.
To the engineer, the glass is twice as big as it needs to be.

The graduate with a Science degree asks, “Why does it work?”
The graduate with an Engineering degree asks, “How does it work?”
The graduate with an Accounting degree asks, “How much will it cost?”
The graduate with a Liberal Arts degree asks, “Do you want fries with that?”

Three lawyers and three engineers are traveling by train to a conference. At the station, the three lawyers each buy tickets and watch as the three engineers buy only a single ticket. “How are three people going to travel on only one ticket?” asked one of the three lawyers. “Watch and you'll see,” answers one of the engineers. They all board the train. The lawyers take their respective seats but all three engineers cram into a restroom and close the door behind them. Shortly after the train has departed, the conductor comes around collecting tickets. He knocks on the restroom door and says, “Ticket, please.” The door opens just a crack and a single arm emerges with a ticket in hand. The conductor takes it and moves on. The lawyers saw this and agreed it was quite a clever idea. So after the conference, the lawyers decide to copy the engineers on the return trip and save some money. When they get to the station, they buy a single ticket for the return trip. To their astonishment, the engineers don't buy a ticket at all. “How are you going to travel without a ticket,” asks one perplexed lawyer. “Watch and you'll see,” says one of the engineers. When they board the train, the three lawyers cram into a restroom and the three engineers cram into another one nearby. The train departs. Shortly afterward, one of the engineers leaves their restroom and walks over to the restroom where the lawyers are hiding. He knocks on the door and says, “Ticket, please.”

A young and beautiful woman gets into the elevator, smelling like expensive perfume. She turns to an old woman and says arrogantly, “Giorgio Beverly Hills, $100 an ounce!” Another beautiful woman gets on the elevator and also smells of very expensive perfume. She arrogantly turns to the old woman and says, “Chanel No. 5, $150 an ounce!” About three floors later, the old woman has reached her destination and is about to get off the elevator. Before she leaves, she looks both beautiful women in the eye, turns, bends over, and farts.. “Broccoli 49 cents a pound.”

A guy goes into a bar. He's sitting on the stool, enjoying his drink when he hears, “You look great!” He looks around - there's nobody near him. He hears the voice again, “No really, you look terrific.” The guy looks around again, Nobody. He hears, “Is that a new shirt or something because you are absolutely glowing!” He then realizes that the voice is coming from a dish of nuts on the bar. “Hey,” the guy calls to the bartender, “What's with the nuts?” “Oh” the bartender answers, “They're complimentary.”

HOW TO IDENTIFY WHERE A DRIVER IS FROM

1. One hand on wheel, one hand on horn: Chicago.
2. One hand on wheel, one finger out window: New York.
3. One hand on wheel, cradling cell phone, brick on accelerator California. (With gun in lap: L.A.)
4. One hand on wheel, one hand on newspaper, foot solidly on the accelerator: Boston.
5. Both hands on wheel, eyes shut, both feet on brake, quivering in terror: Ohio, but driving in California.
6. Both hands in air, gesturing, both feet on accelerator, head turned around to talk to someone in back seat: Italy.
7. One hand on latte, one knee on wheel, cradling cell phone, foot on brake, mind on game: Seattle.
8. One hand on wheel, one hand on hunting rifle, alternating between both feet being on the accelerator and both on the brake, throwing a McDonalds bag out the window: Texas
9. Four wheel drive pickup truck, shotgun mounted in rear window, beer cans on floor, squirrel tails attached to antenna: West Virginia
10. Two hands gripping wheel, blue hair barely visible above window level, driving 35 on the interstate in the left lane with the left blinker on: Florida

Bud and Jim were a couple of drinking buddies who worked as airplane mechanics in L.A. One day the airport was fogged in and they were stuck in the hangar with nothing to do. Bud said, “Man, I wish we had something to drink!” Jim says, “You know, I've heard you can drink jet fuel and get a buzz. You wanna try it?” So they pour themselves a couple of glasses of high octane hooch and get completely smashed. The next morning Bud wakes up and is surprised at how great he feels and no hangover and no bad side effects. Then the phone rings ...It's Jim and he says, “Hey, how do you feel this morning?" Bud says, "I feel great." Jim says "I feel great, too. You don't have a hangover?" Bud says, "No, that jet fuel is great stuff no hangover at all. We ought to do this more often." Jim said "Yeah, well there's just one thing..." "What's that" Bud asked. "Have you farted yet?" "No." "Well, DON'T, 'cause I'm in PHOENIX!!!"

Food Wisdom

1. If you eat something and no one sees you eat it, it has no calories.
2. If you drink a diet soda with a candy bar, the calories in the candy bar are cancelled out by the diet soda.
3. When you eat with someone else, calories don't count if you don't eat more than they do.
4. Food used for medicinal purposes NEVER count, such as hot chocolate, brandy, toast and Sara Lee Cheesecake.
5. If you fatten up everyone else around you, then you look thinner.
6. Movie related foods (Milk Duds, Buttered Popcorn, Junior Mints, Tootsie Rolls etc.) do not have additional calories because they are part of the entertainment package and not part of one's personal fuel.
7. Foods that are frozen have no calories because calories are units of heat. Examples are ice cream, frozen pies, and Popsicles.
8. Things licked off knives and spoons have no calories if you are in the process of preparing something. Examples are peanut butter on a knife making a sandwich and ice cream on a spoon making a sundae.
9. Foods that have the same color have the same number of calories. Examples are: spinach and pistachio ice cream; mushrooms and white chocolate. NOTE: Chocolate is a universal color and may be substituted for any other food color.
10. Cookie pieces contain no fat--the process of breaking causes fat leakage.

An Illinois man left the snowballed streets of Chicago for a vacation in Florida. His wife was on a business trip and was planning to meet him there the next day. When he reached his hotel, he decided to send his wife a quick e-mail. Unable to find the scrap of paper on which he had written her e-mail address, he did his best to type it in from memory. Unfortunately, he missed one letter and his note was directed instead to an elderly preacher's wife, whose husband had passed away only the day before. When the grieving widow checked her e-mail, she took one look at the monitor, let out a piercing scream, and fell to the floor dead. At the sound, her family rushed into the room and saw this note on the screen: Dearest Wife, Just got checked in. Everything prepared for your arrival tomorrow. Your Loving Husband. PS: Sure is hot down here.

A successful businessman flew to Vegas for the weekend to gamble. He lost the shirt off his back, and had nothing left but a quarter and the second half of his round trip ticket -- If he could just get to the airport he could get himself home. So he went out to the front of the casino where there was a cab waiting. He got in and explained his situation to the cabbie. He promised to send the driver money from home, he offered him his credit card numbers, his drivers license number, his address, etc, but to no avail. The cabbie said “If you don't have fifteen dollars, get the hell out of my cab!” So the businessman was forced to hitch-hike to the airport and was barely in time to catch his flight. One year later the businessman, having worked long and hard to regain his financial success, returned to Vegas and this time he won big. Feeling pretty good about himself, he went out to the front of the casino to get a cab ride back to the airport. Well who should he see out there, at the end of a long line of cabs, but his old buddy who had refused to give him a ride when he was down on his luck. The businessman thought for a moment about how he could make the guy pay for his lack of charity, and he hit on a plan. The businessman got in the first cab in the line, “How much for a ride to the airport,” he asked? "Fifteen bucks," came the reply. "And how much for you to give me a blowjob on the way?" "What?! Get the hell out of my cab." The businessman got into the back of each cab in the long line and asked the same questions, with the same result. When he got to his old friend at the back of the line, he got in and asked "How much for a ride to the airport?" The cabbie replied "fifteen bucks." The businessman said "ok" and off they went. Then, as they drove slowly past the long line of cabs the businessman gave a big smile and thumbs up sign to each driver.

A man is doing yard work and his wife is about to take a shower. The man realizes that he can't find the rake. He yells up to his wife, "Where is the rake?" She can't hear him and shouts back, "What?" The man first points to his eye, then points to his knee and finally makes a raking motion. The wife is not sure and says, "What?' and the man repeats his gestures. "EYE KNEE THE RAKE" The wife replies that she understands and signals back. She first points to her eye, next she points to her left breast, then she points to her butt, and finally to her crotch. Well, there is no way in hell the man can even come close on that one. Exasperated, he goes upstairs and asks "What the hell was that?" She replies, "EYE - LEFT TIT - BEHIND - THE BUSH

<u>REAL SIGNS</u>

1. In a Laundromat - Automatic washing machines. Please all your clothes when the light goes out.
2. In a London department story -Bargain Basement Upstairs
3. In an office - Would the person who took the step ladder yesterday please bring it back or further steps will be taken.
4. In another office - After the tea break staff should empty the teapot and stand upside down on the draining board.
5. On a church door - This is the gate of Heaven. Enter ye all by this door. (This door is kept locked because of the draft. Please use side entrance)

6. OUTSIDE A SECOND HAND SHOP: We exchange anything bicycles, washing machines etc. Why not bring your wife along and get a wonderful bargain.

7. QUICKSAND WARNING: Quicksand. Any person passing this point will be drowned. By order of the District Council.

8. NOTICE IN A DRY CLEANER'S WINDOW: Anyone leaving their garments here for more than 30 days will be disposed of.

9. IN A HEALTH FOOD SHOP WINDOW: Closed due to illness.

10. IN A SAFARI PARK: Elephants Please Stay In Your Car

11. SEEN DURING A CONFERENCE: For anyone who has children and doesn't know it, there is a day care on the first floor.

12. NOTICE IN A FIELD: The farmer allows walkers to cross the field for free, but the bull charges.

13. MESSAGE ON A LEAFLET: If you cannot read, this leaflet will tell you how to get lessons.

14. ON A REPAIR SHOP DOOR: We can repair anything (Please knock hard on the door - the bell doesn't work)

15. SPOTTED IN A TOILET IN A LONDON OFFICE BLOCK: Toilet out of order. Please use floor below.

Since we have to speak well of the dead, let's knock them while they're alive.

Bumper Stickers:

1. Honk if you've never seen an Uzi fired from a car window
2. Fight Crime: Shoot Back!
3. If you can read this, please flip me back over... (seen upside down, on a Jeep)
4. Remember folks: Stop lights timed for 35 mph are also timed for 70 mph.
5. If walking is so good for you, then why does my mailman look like Jabba the Hutt??
6. Heart Attacks.. .God's Revenge For Eating His Animal Friends
7. We have enough youth, how about a fountain of smart?
8. Boldly going nowhere
9. Cat: The other white meat
10. Eat Well, Stay Fit, Die Anyway
11. He's not dead, He's electroencephalographically challenged
12. If at first you don't succeed, skydiving is not for you
13. If you can't dazzle them with brilliance, riddle them with bullets
14. If you lived in your car, you'd be home by now
15. WARNING! Driver only carries $20.00 in ammunition

Arthur Davidson, of the Harley Davidson Motorcycle Corporation, dies and goes to heaven. At the gates, an angel tells Davidson, "Well, you've been such a good guy and your motorcycles have changed the world. As a reward, you can hang out with anyone you want to in Heaven." Davidson thinks about it and says, "I wanna hang out with God, Himself.". The feathered fellow at the Gates takes Arthur to the Throne Room and introduces him to God. Arthur then asks God, "Hey, aren't you the inventor of Woman?" God says, "Ah, yes." "Well, says Davidson, "You have some major design flaws in your invention: There's too much front end protrusion; it chatters at high speeds; the rear end wobbles too much, and the intake is placed too close to the exhaust." "Hmmm" replies God, "Hold on." God goes to the

Celestial Supercomputer, types in a few keystrokes, and waits for the result. The computer prints out a slip of paper and God reads it. "It may be that my invention is flawed," God replies to Arthur Davidson, "but according to my computer, more men are riding my invention than yours."

Two very elderly ladies were enjoying the sunshine on a park bench in Miami. They had been meeting at that park every sunny day for over 12 years, chatting, and enjoying each other's friendship. One day the younger of the two turns to the other and says, "Please don't be angry with me, dear, but I am embarrassed, after all these years. What is your name? I am trying to remember, but I just can't." The older friend stares at her, looking very distressed, says nothing for two full minutes, and finally says, "How soon do you have to know?"

For the first time in many years, an old man traveled from his rural town to the city to attend a movie. After buying his ticket, he stopped at the concession stand to purchase some popcorn. Handing the attendant $1.50, he couldn't help but comment, "The last time I came to the movies, popcorn was only 15 cents." "Well, sir," the attendant replied with a grin, "You're really going to enjoy yourself, we have sound now."

A truck driver hauling a tractor-trailer load of computers stops for a cold one. As he approaches the bar he sees a big sign on the door saying "NERDS NOT ALLOWED - ENTER AT YOUR OWN RISK!" He goes in and sits down. The bartender comes over to him, sniffs, says he smells kind of nerdy, and asks him what he does for a living. The truck driver says he drives a truck, and the smell is just from the computers he is hauling. The bartender says OK, truck drivers are not nerds, and serves him a beer. As he is sipping his brew, a skinny guy walks in with tape around his glasses, a pocket protector with twelve kinds of pens and pencils, and a belt at least a foot too long. The bartender, without saying a word, pulls out a shotgun and blows the guy away. The truck driver asks him why he did that. The bartender said not to worry, the nerds are over-populating the Silicon Valley, and are in season now. You don't even need a license, he said. So the truck driver finishes his beer, gets back in his truck, and heads back onto the freeway. Suddenly he veers to avoid an accident, and the load shifts. The back door breaks open and computers spill out all over the freeway. He jumps out and sees a crowd already forming, grabbing up the computers. They are all engineers, accountants and programmers wearing the nerdiest clothes he has ever seen. He can't let them steal his whole load. So remembering what happened in the bar, he pulls out his gun and starts blasting away, felling several of them instantly. A highway patrol officer comes zooming up and jumps out of the car screaming at him to stop. The truck driver said, “What's wrong? I thought nerds were in season.” “Well, sure.” said the patrolman, “But you can't bait 'em.

A man walks into a bar with an ostrich and a cat and sits at the bar. The bartender walks over to them and says, “What can I get for you?” The man says, “I'll have a beer”, the ostrich says “I'll have a beer” and the cat says “I'll have half a beer and I'm not buying.” So the bartender says, “OK, that will be $3.87” The man reaches into his pocket and brings out the exact change and pays him. About an hour later the bartender goes back over to them and says, “What'll you guys have?” The man says, “I'll have a beer”, the ostrich says “I'll have a beer” and the cat says “I'll have half a beer and I'm not buying.” The bartender gets them their beer and says, “That'll be $3.87.” The man reaches into his pocket and brings out the exact change and pays him. A couple of days later they come back into the bar and the bartender walks over and asks, “What do you guys want today?” The man says, “I'll have a scotch”, the ostrich says, “I'll have a bourbon” and the cat says, “I'll have half a beer and I'm not buying.” So the bartender says “OK, that will be $7.53.”. The man reaches into his pocket and brings out the exact change and pays him. The bartender's curiosity got the best of him and he asks, “Why is it that every time I tell you the amount you owe you always have the exact change in your pocket?” The man said, “I found a bottle with a genie in it and she granted me 3 wishes. My first wish was that I always have the exact change in my pocket for anything I buy.” The bartender says, “That's a great wish ...better than asking for a million dollars. A million dollars will run out but that never will. What were your other 2 wishes?” The man says, “That's where I screwed up. I asked for a chick with long legs and a tight pussy.

Before going to Europe on business, a man drove his Rolls-Royce to a downtown New York City bank and went in to ask for an immediate loan of $5,000. The loan officer, taken aback, requested collateral and so the man said, “Well then, here are the keys to my Rolls-Royce.” The loan officer promptly had the car driven into the bank's underground parking for safe keeping, and gave him $5,000. Two weeks later, the man walked through the bank's doors, and asked to settle up his loan and get his car back. “That will be $5,000 in principal, and $15.40 in interest”, the loan officer said. The man wrote out a check and started to walk away. “Wait sir”, the loan officer said, “I found out you are a millionaire. Why would you need to borrow $5,000?” The man smiled. “Where else could I park in Manhattan for two weeks and pay only $15.40?

What has four legs and an arm? A happy pit bull

A REDNECK LOVE POEM
Collards is green, my dog's name is Blue
And I'm so lucky to have a sweet thang like you.

Yore hair is like corn silk a-flapping in the breeze.
Softer than Blue's and without all them fleas.

You move like the bass, which excite me in May.
You ain't got no scales but I luv you anyway.

You're as satisfy'n as okry jist a-fry'n in the pan.
Yore as fragrant as "snuff' right out of the can.

You have some'a yore teeth, for which I am proud
I hold my head high when we're in a crowd.

On special occasions, when you shave under yore arms
Well, I'm in hawg heaven, and awed by yore charms.

Still them fellers at work, they all want to know
What I did to deserve such a purdy, young doe.

Like a good roll of duct tape yore there fer yore man
To patch up life's troubles and fix what you can.

Yore as cute as a junebug a-buzzin' overhead
You ain't mean like those far ants I found in my bed.

Cut from the best cloth like a plaid flannel shirt
You spark up my life more than a fresh load of dirt.

When you hold me real tight like a padded gun rack
My life is complete; Ain't nuttin' I lack.

Yore complexion, it's perfection, like the best vinyl sidin'.
Despite all the years, yore age, it keeps hidin'.

Me 'n' you's like a Moon Pie with a RC cold drank
We go together like a skunk goes with stank.

Some men, they buy chocolate for Valentine's Day
They git it at Wal-Mart, it's romantic that way.

Some men git roses on that special day
From the cooler at Kroger. "That's impressive," I say.

Some men buy fine diamonds from a flea market booth.
"Diamonds are forever," they explain, suave and couth.

But for this man, honey, these won't do.
Cause yore too special, you sweet thang you.

I got you a gift, without taste nor odor,
more useful than diamonds it's a new troll'n motor!!

<u>HILLBILLY DICTIONARY</u>

LOG ON: Making a wood stove hot.
LOG OFF: Don't add no more wood.
MONITOR: Keeping an eye on the woodstove.
DOWNLOAD: Gittin the farwood off the truck.
MEGA HERTZ: When you're not keerfull gittin the farwood.
FLOPPY DISC: Whatcha git from trying to tote too much farwood.
RAM: That thar thing whut splits the farwood.
HARD DRIVE: Gitting home in the winter time.
WINDOWS: Whut to shut when it's cold outside.
SCREEN: Whut to shut when it's black fly season.
BYTE: Whut dem dang flies do.
CHIP: Munchies fer the TV.
MICRO CHIP: Whut's in the bottom of the munchie bag.
MODEM: Whatcha do to the hay fields.
DOT MATRIX: Old Dan Matrix's wife.
LAP 'TOP: Whar the kitty sleeps.
KEYBOARD: Whar you hang the dang truck keys.
SOFTWARE: Them dang plastic forks and knifes.
MOUSE: What eats the grain in the barn.
MOUSE PAD: That's hippie talk fer the mouse home.
MAINFRAME: Holds up the barn roof.
PORT: Fancy Flatlander wine.
ENTER: Northerner talk fer, "C'mon in y'all".
CLICK: Whut you hear when you cock your gun.
DOUBLE CLICK: When the dang gun don't far when you pull the trigger.

REBOOT: Whut you have to do right before bedtime when you forgot the kitty's still outside.

Q. How many rednecks does it take to eat a possum?
A. Three, one to eat the possum and two to watch for cars.

This guy was deer hunting in North Carolina. He shoots a deer, and as he is dragging it back to his truck, he gets stopped by this redneck Game Warden who asks to see his hunting license. The hunter shows him the license, and is about to leave when the Game Warden says “Not so fast, Boy. I need to inspect the deer.” The Game Warden then reaches down, sticks his finger up the deer's butt, pulls it out then sniffs his finger. The Game Warden gets angry then says “Wait a minute Boy! This here ain't no North Carolina deer; this here is a Virginia deer! You need to have a Virginia Hunting License to hunt this deer. You got a Virginia Hunting License on you Boy?” Well, it just so happens that the guy had been hunting in Virginia the week before. He goes back into his wallet hand pulls out a Virginia Hunting License. The Game Warden looks at the valid license and disappointingly says, “Well.... OK, I guess I'll have to let you go. I really do enjoy writing up Boys like you who hunt deer without a license, but you look like you got everything in order. So go on; get out of here.” The following week, the guy is hunting again. He shoots another deer and as he is dragging it back to his truck, he gets stopped by the same Game Warden who says “Just a minute Boy. I need to inspect the deer.” He reaches down, sticks his finger up the deer's butt, pulls it out, sniffs his finger and says “Boy! This here is a South Carolina deer! You got a South Carolina Hunting License?” The Hunter, somewhat surprised, said that he had one in the truck. He goes and gets it out of the glove box, shows it to the Game Warden, who again has to let him go. So this goes on for the next three weeks. Each week the hunter shoots a deer; one from Georgia, Tennessee, and West Virginia. Each time the Game Warden stops to do the Finger Test, and each time the hunter is able to produce the correct license. Finally, after the West Virginia deer, the Game Warden is furious: "Boy! You got a hunting license from every state in the south! Where the hell are you from, anyway?" The hunter drops his pants, bends over and says "You Tell Me!"

A hillbilly man and his new bride were on their honeymoon. The husband jumps into bed to wait for his wife to get herself ready. The wife comes out of the bathroom in a sexy negligee and says "Honey, I have something to tell you. I'm a virgin." The man grabs his clothes and heads straight to his fathers house. The son says, "My new wife told me a big secret of hers. She's a virgin." "Damn son. You did the right thing by leaving. If she wasn't good enough for her family, she sure as hell isn't good enough for ours!"

<u>TOP 25 COUNTRY SONGS</u>

25. Get Your Tongue Outta My Mouth 'Cause I'm Kissing You Goodbye.
24. Her Teeth Was Stained, But Her Heart Was Pure.
23. How Can I Miss You If You Won't Go Away?
22. I Don't Know Whether To Kill Myself Or Go Bowling.
21. I Just Bought A Car From A Guy That Stole My Girl, But The Car Don't Run So I Figure We Got An Even Deal.
20. I Keep Forgettin' I Forgot About You.
19. 1 Liked You Better Before I Knew You So Well.
18. I Still Miss You, Baby, But My Aim's Gettin' Better.
17. I Wouldn't Take Her To A Dog Fight, Cause I'm Afraid She'd Win.
16. I'll Marry You Tomorrow But Let's Honeymoon Tonight.
15. I'm So Miserable Without You, It's Like Having You Here.
14. I've Got Tears In My Ears From Lyin' On My Back and Cryin' Over You.
13. If I Can't Be Number One In Your Life, Then Number "Two On You.
12. If I Had Shot You When I Wanted To, I'd Be Out By Now.

11. Mama Get A Hammer (There's A Fly On Papa's Head).
10. My Head Hurts, My Feet Stink, And I Don't Love You.
9. My Wife Ran Off With My Best Friend, I Sure Do Miss Him.
8. Please Bypass This Heart.
7. She Got The Ring And I Got The Finger.
6. You Done Tore Out My Heart And Stomped That Sucker Flat.
5. You're The Reason Our Kids Are So Ugly.
4. If The Phone Don't Ring, You'll Know It's Me.
3. She's Actin' Single and I'm Drinkin' Doubles.
2. She's Looking Better After Every Beer.
1. I Haven't Gone To Bed With Any Ugly Women But I've Sure Woke Up With A Few.

YOU JUST MIGHT BE A YANKEE IF:

1. You think barbecue is a verb meaning "to cook outside."
2. You think Heinz Ketchup is really SPICY!
3. You don't have any problems pronouncing "Worcestershire sauce" correctly.
4. For breakfast, you would prefer potatoes au gratin to grits.
5. You don't know what a moon pie is.
6. You've never had an RC cola.
7. You've never, ever, eaten okra, fried or boiled.
8. You eat fried chicken with a knife and fork.
9. You've never seen a live chicken, and the only cows you've seen are on road trips.
10. You have no idea what a polecat is.
11. You don't see anything wrong with putting a sweater on a poodle.
12. You don't have bangs.
13. You would rather vacation at Martha's Vineyard than Six Flags.
14. More than two generations of your family have been kicked out of the same prep school.
15. You would rather have your son become a lawyer than get his own TV fishing show.
16. Instead of referring to two or more people as "y'all," you

call them “you guys,” even if both of them are women.

17. You don't think Ted Kennedy has an accent.
18. You don't have any hats in your closet that advertise feed stores.
19. You think more money should go to important scientific research at your university than to pay the salary of the head football coach.
20. You don't have at least one can of WD-40 somewhere around the house.
21. The last time you smiled was when you prevented someone from getting on an on-ramp to the highway.
22. You have never planned your summer vacation around a gun-knife show.
23. The farthest south you've ever been is the perfume counter at Neiman Marcus.
24. You call binoculars opera glasses.
25. You can't spit out the car window without pulling over to the side of the road and stopping.
26. You would never wear pink or an appliqué sweatshirt.
27. You don't know what appliqué is.
28. You don't know anyone with at least two first names (i.e., Joe Bob, Billy Ray, Mary Jo, Bubba Dean, Mary Alice, et al).
29. You don't have doilies, and you certainly don't know how to make one.
30. You've never been to a craft show.
31. You get freaked out when people on the subway talk to you.
32. You can do your laundry without quarters.
33. None of your fur coats are homemade.

The following short quiz consists of 4 questions and test whether you tend to do simple things in an overly complicated way. Remember, the questions are not that difficult

1. Q. How do you put a giraffe into a refrigerator?
Correct Answer. Open the refrigerator, put in the giraffe and close the door.

2. Q. How do you put an elephant into a refrigerator?
Wrong Answer: Open the refrigerator, put in the elephant and close the refrigerator.
Correct Answer: Open the refrigerator, take out the giraffe, put in the elephant and close the door.

3. Q. The Lion King is hosting an animal conference, all the animals attend except one. Which animal does not attend?
Correct Answer: The Elephant because it is in the refrigerator.

4. Q. There is a river you must cross. But it is inhabited by crocodiles. How do you manage it?
Correct Answer: You swim across. All the Crocodiles are attending the Animal Meeting!

Farmer Jake had a nagging wife who made his life miserable. The only real peace that he got was when he was out in the field plowing. One day when he was out in the field, Jake's wife brought his lunch to him. Then she stayed while he quietly ate and berated him with a constant stream of nagging and complaining. Suddenly, Jake's old mule kicked up his back legs, striking the wife in the head, and killing her instantly. At the wake, Jake's minister noticed that when the women offered their sympathy to Jake he would nod his head up and down, but when the men came up and spoke quietly to him, he would shake his head from side to side. When the wake was over and all the mourners had left, the minister approached Jake and asked, “Why was it that you nodded your head up and down to all the women and shook your head from side to side to all the men?” “Well,” Jake replied, “The women all said how nice she looked, and her dress was so pretty, so I agreed by nodding my head up and down. The men all asked, “Is that mule for sale?” and I shook my head, no.

How to identify a person by their farts:

1. AMBITIOUS - Always ready for a fart.
2. LAZY - Just fizzles.
3. AMIABLE - Likes to smell others' farts (needs therapy).
4. SELFISH - Only enjoys smelling his own farts.
5. CARELESS - Farts in church.
6. SMART ALEC - Farts in the presence of ladies and old people.
7. CLEVER - Coughs and farts at the same time.
8. SCIENTIFIC - Bottles his farts and donates them to the University.
9. STINGY - Belches instead of farts to save his butt hole.
10. TIMID - Jumps when he farts, then cries.
11. SHY - Blushes as he farts silently.
12. CONCEITED - Thinks he can fart the loudest and tries.
13. UNLUCKY - Tries to fart, can't, oops, present in the shorts.
14. FOOLISH - Farts and giggles.
15. BEWILDERED - Can't tell his own from others.
16. SLOVENLY - Farts and fizzles, rots his pants
17. NERVOUS - Stops in the middle of a fart.
18. MISERABLE - Can't fart at all. Gains much girth.
19. GROUCH - Grumbles when ladies fart.
20. CONFUSED - Face is so much like a butt, fart can't tell which way to go.
21. SNEAKY - Farts and blames it on the dog.
22. DISAPPOINTED - One whose farts don't smell.
23. FRESH GUY - Jumps in front of you to fart.
24. BULLY - Farts louder than anyone else.
25. DELUDED - Enjoys other farts, thinking they are his own.
26. ANALYTICAL - Discovers from farts what was eaten.
27. WISEASS - Farts and asks, "Who in the hell pooped?"
28. MEAN - Farts in bed -- pulls sheet over spouse's head.
29. MUSICAL - Tenor or bass, clear as a bell, smells like poop and sounds like hell.
30. HONEST - Admits that it was the hostess who farted.
31. LONELY GUY - Jumps in the air, farts three times, and

clicks his heels simultaneously.

32. DISHONEST - Is so good at convincing others that he didn't fart that others begin to feel bad, even though they KNOW it was him.
33. SLY - Farts in a crowd, then quietly looks around to see the looks on other's faces as the reek reaches them.
34. RANGER - See SLY, but also looks to see how far they travel by the looks on peoples faces.

Bill walks into a bar and sees Bob sitting at the end of the bar counter with a great big smile on his face. Bill says, “Bob, what are you so happy for?” “Well Bill, I gotta tell ya...yesterday I was out waxing' my boat and a redhead came up to me…boobs out to here. She says 'Can I have a ride in your boat?' I said, 'Sure you can have a ride in my boat.' So I took her way out, Bill. I turned off the key and I said 'Its either screw or swim!' She couldn't swim, Bill!” The next day Bill walks into the bar and sees Bob sitting at the end of the bar counter with a Bigger smile on his face. Bill says “What are you so happy about today, Bob?” “Well Bill... I gotta tell ya... Yesterday I was out waxing' my boat and a BEAUTIFUL blonde came up to me... boobs out to here. She said, 'Can I have a ride in your boat?' 'Sure you can have a ride in my boat.' So I took her way out, Bill, way out much further than the last one. I turned off the key and I said 'It's either screw or swim!' She couldn't swim!” A couple days pass and Bill walks into the bar and sees Bob down there crying' over a beer. Bill says, “Bob, what are you so sad for?” “Well Bill, I gotta tell ya....yesterday I was out waxing' my boat and the most desirable brunette came up to me...boobs WAY out to here, Bill. She says, 'Can I have a ride in your boat?' 'Sure you can have a ride in my boat.' So I took her way out, Bill, way WAY, out. ..much further than the last two. I turned off the key, and looked at her boobs and said, 'It's either screw or swim!!'. She seductively pulled down her pants, and.... she had a penis, Bill!! She had a great big penis!!! And Bill... I CAN'T SWIM.”

A traveling salesman had been on the road for two months and was finally on his way home. Feeling bad about having been away from his children so long, he decided to buy them a gift. So he stopped by a pet store and bought them a cute little puppy. Unfortunately, he was stopped on his way in by a stewardess who told him, "I'm sorry sir, but we don't allow animals." In desperation, the man popped into the men's room and stuffed the puppy down the front of his pants, and put his overcoat on to cover up. Then he reboarded the plane. The plane took off, and a half-hour later, the stewardess was making her rounds when she noticed that the salesman was looking pale and fidgeting in his seat. She asked if he was alright, and he said that he was just feeling a little airsick. However, fifteen minutes later, she noticed that he was sweating and squirming his seat. The stewardess came back and asked again if the salesman was alright. He answered, "Well, actually, you know that puppy that you said I couldn't bring on the plane? I stuffed it in my pants and brought it onboard anyway." "But sir," said the stewardess. "Why do you look so ill?" "Well, apparently the darned thing isn't weaned yet."

Daffynitions

Avoidable \uh-voy'-duh-buhl\: What a bullfighter tries to do.
Baloney \buh-lo'-nee\: Where some hemlines fall.
Bernadette \burn'-a-det\:The act of torching a mortgage.
Burglarize \bur'-gler-ize\:What a crook sees with.
Counterfeiters\kown-ter-fit-ers\:Workers installing kitchen cabinet.
Eclipse \e-klips'\:What an English barber does for a living.
Eyedropper \i'-drop-ur\:A clumsy ophthalmologist.
Heroes \hee'-rhos\:What a guy in a boat does.
Left Bank \left' bangk'\: What the robber did when his bag was full of loot.
Misty \mis'-tee\:How golfers create divots.
Paradox \par'-uh-doks\:Two physicians.
Parasites \par'-uh-sites\: What you see from the top of the Eiffel Tower.

Pharmacist \farm'-uh-sist\:A helper on the farm.
Polarize \po'-lur-ize\: What penguins see with.

Three Marines were walking through the forest when they came upon a set of tracks. The first Marine said, “Those are deer tracks.” The second Marine said, “No, those are elk tracks.” The third Marine said “You're both wrong, those are moose tracks.” The Marines were still arguing when the train hit them.

An Amish boy and his father were visiting a mall. They were amazed by almost everything they saw, but especially by two shiny, silver walls that could move apart and then slide back together again. The boy asked, “What is this, Father?” The father (never having seen an elevator) responded, Son, I have never seen anything like this in my life, I don't know what it is. While the boy and his father were watching with amazement, a fat old lady in a wheel chair rolled up to the moving walls and pressed a button. The walls opened and the lady rolled between them into a small room. The walls closed and the boy and his father watched the small circular numbers above the walls light up sequentially. They continued to watch until it reached the last number and then the numbers began to light in the reverse order. Finally the walls opened up again and a gorgeous, voluptuous 24 year old blonde woman stepped out. The father, not taking his eyes off the young woman, said quietly to his son.. Go get your mother.”

<u>Things to say before firing a person:</u>
I don't know what we'll do without you, but we are going to try!

Today I'm going to mix business with pleasure. You're fired!

We told everyone you are leaving because of illness. The truth is I'm sick of you.

Tell me, how long have you been with us not counting tomorrow?

Its not that you aren't a responsible worker. In fact, you've been responsible for more disasters than any one else in the place.

I've got good news for you. You won't have to worry about being late for work ever again.

They told me to get some enthusiasm back into this unit. So I'm firing you with enthusiasm.

A drunk stumbles along a Baptismal service on a Sunday afternoon down by the river. He proceeds to stumble down into the water and stands next to the Minister. The Minister turns, notices the old drunk and says, "Mister, are you ready to find Jesus?" The drunk looks back and says, "Yes sir, I am." The Minister then dunks the fellow under the water and pulls him right back up. "Have you found Jesus?" the Minister asked. "No, I didn't!" said the drunk.
The Minister then dunks him under for a quite a bit longer, brings him up and says, "Now brother, have you found Jesus?" "No, I did not!" said the drunk again. Disgusted, the Minister holds the man under for at least 30 seconds this time, brings him up and demands, "For the grace of God, have you found Jesus yet? The old drunk wipes his eyes and pleads, "Are you sure this is where he fell in?"

The Dieter's Prayer:

My appetite is my shepherd, I always want.
It maketh me sit down and stuff myself.
It leadeth me to my refrigerator repeatedly
Sometimes during the night.
It leadeth me in the path of Burger King for a Whopper.
It destroyeth my shape.
Yea, though I knoweth I gaineth, I will not stop eating,
For the food tasteth so good.

The ice cream and the cookies, they comfort me.
When the table is spread before me, it exciteth me.
For I knoweth that I sooneth shall dig in.
As I filleth my plate continuously.
My clothes runneth smaller.
Surely bulges and pudgies shall follow me
All the days of my life
And I shall be “pleasingly plump” forever.

<u>The Beer Drinker's Prayer:</u>

Our lager, Which art in barrels,
Hallowed be thy drink.
I will be drunk, At home as in the tavern.
Give us this day our foamy head,
And forgive us our spillages,
As we forgive those who spill against us.
And lead us not to incarceration,
But deliver us from hangovers.
For thine is the beer,
The bitter and The lager.
Forever and ever.
Barmen

Forrest Gump died and went to heaven. When he got to the Pearly Gate Saint Peter told him that new rules were in effect due to the advances in education on earth. In order to gain admittance a prospective heavenly soul must answer three questions.

1. Name two days of the week that begin with “T”.
2. How many seconds are in a year?
3. What's God's first name?

Forrest thought for a few minutes and answered.

#1. The two days of the week that begin with “T” are Today and Tomorrow.”

#2. There are 12 seconds in a year.”

#3. God has two first names and they are Andy and Howard.”

Saint Peter said, "OK I'll buy Today and Tomorrow, even though it's not the answer I expected, your answer is correct. But how did you get 12 seconds in a year and why did you ever think that God's first name was either Andy or Howard?" Forrest responded, "Well, January 2nd, February 2nd, March 2nd, etc...." "OK, I give you that one," said Saint Peter, "but what about the God's first name stuff?" Forrest said, "Well, from the song... Andy walks with me, Andy talks with me, Andy tells me I am his own... and the prayer... Our Father who art in Heaven Howard be thy name...." Saint Peter let him in without further ado.

Q. What do you call a virgin on a waterbed?
A. A cherry float.

Q. If there is H20 on the inside of a fire hydrant, what is on the outside?
A. K9P.

Q. What did the sign on the door of the whorehouse say?
A. Beat it - we're closed.

Q. Why do walruses go to Tupperware parties?
A. To find a tight seal.

Q. What do you do with 365 used rubbers?
A. Melt them down, make a tire, and call it a Goodyear.

Q. What's the difference between sin and shame?
A. It is a sin to put it in, but it's a shame to pull it out.

Q. What's the speed limit of sex?
A. 68; at 69 you eat it.

Q. How far can you have sex?
A. 68 miles, at 69 you have to turn around.

Q. What's the ultimate rejection?
A. When you're masturbating and your hand falls asleep.

Q. Why did Raggedy Ann get thrown out of the toy box?
A. She kept sitting on Pinocchio's face, and moaning, "Lie to me!"

Q. Why is air a lot like sex?
A. Because it's no big deal unless you're not getting any.

Q. What's another name for pickled bread?
A. Dill-dough

Mr. Smith got himself a new secretary. She was young, sweet, and very polite. One day while taking dictation, she noticed his fly was open. When leaving the room, she said, "Mr. Smith, your barracks door is open." He did not understand her remark. But, later on, he happened to look down and saw his zipper was open. He decided to have some fun with secretary. Calling her in, he asked, "By the way, Miss Jones, when you saw my barracks door open this morning, did you also notice a soldier standing at attention?" The secretary, who was quite witty, replied, "Why, no sir. All I saw was a little disabled veteran sitting on two duffel bags."

A businessman on his deathbed called his friend and said, "Bill, I want you to promise me that when I die you will have my remains cremated." "And what," his friend asked, "do you want me to do with your ashes?" The businessman said, "Just put them in an envelope and mail them to the Internal Revenue Service and write on the envelope, "Now you have everything."

A really fat man got out of the shower at the health club. A second man said, "Gee, you're fat, how long has it been since you've seen your dick?" The fat man answered, "A long time." The second man asked, "Why don't you diet?" The fat man asks, "Why? What color is it now?"

Q. How do you get a doper to stop rolling joints?
A. Cut off his fingers.

Q. Why do women have foreheads?
A. So we have a place to kiss them after we come in their mouths.

Q. What should you do if a girl sits on your hand?
A. Try to get her off.

Q. Why do men have faces?
A. So the girls can recognize which prick is theirs.

Q. How can you tell if a woman really likes oral sex?
A. She hikes up her skirt every time someone yawns. Buford goes to the doctor and says, "Doc, you've gotta help me. I eat apples, apples come out. I eat bananas, bananas come out." The doctor says, "It's easy. Eat shit."

Three women, a brunette, a redhead, and a blonde, all come home from work at the same time and get on the elevator. The brunette notices a blob on the elevator wall and says "Ooooohhh that looks like semen." She reaches out and touches the blob with her fingers and says "It feels like semen." The redhead reaches out and touches it with her fingers, smells it, and says "It smells like semen." Judi, the blonde, reaches out and touches it with her fingers and then puts her fingers in her mouth and tastes it and says, "It doesn't taste like anyone in this building..."

<u>More Daffynitions</u>
Antacid: Uncle Acid's wife.
Antelope: How she married my Uncle.
Arbitrator: A cook that leaves Arby's to work at McDonald's.
Bottom: What the shopper did when she found the shoes that she wanted.

Bucktooth: The going rate for the tooth fairy.
Cantaloupe: When you are unable to run away to get married.
Cartoonist: What you call your auto mechanic.
Castanets: What they did to fill the role of Frankie Avalon's movie girlfriend.
Celtics: What a parasite salesman does.
Concert: A breath mint for inmates.
Consist: A growth on an inmate.
Content: A fabric shelter for inmates.
Control: A short, ugly inmate.
Convent: How inmates get air conditioning.
Crestfallen: Dropped toothpaste.
Cross-eyed Teacher: A teacher that loses control over her pupils.
Decrease: De fold in de pants.
Demote: What de king put around de castle.
Despise: De persons who work for the CIA.
Detention: What causes de stress.
Dictator: Another name for Richard Spud.
Dilate: When a person lives longer.
Dioxin: What you say before you kill a herd of buffalo-like cattle.
Dreadlocks: the fear of opening the dead-bolt.

A blonde, female, gynecologist, had a burning desire to change careers and become a mechanic. So she found out from her local tech college what was involved, signed up for evening classes and attended diligently, learning all she could. When time for the practical exam approached, she prepared carefully for weeks, and completed the exam with tremendous skill. When the results came back, she was surprised to find that she had obtained a mark of 150%. Fearing an error, she called the instructor, saying "I don't want to appear ungrateful for such an outstanding result, but I wondered if there had been an error which needed adjusting." The instructor said, "During the exam, you took the engine apart perfectly, which was worth 50% of the total mark. You put the engine back together again perfectly, which is also worth 50% of the mark. I gave you an extra 50% because you did all of it THROUGH the muffler..."

When I stopped the bus to pick up Chris for preschool, I noticed an older woman hugging him as he left the house. "Is that your grandmother?" I asked. "Yes," Chris said. "She's come to visit us for Christmas." "How nice," I said. "Where does she live?" "At the airport," Chris replied. "Whenever we want her, we just go out there and get her."

A woman has the last word in any argument. Anything a man says after that, is the beginning of a new argument.

The math teacher saw that little Johnny wasn't paying attention in class. She called on him and said, "Johnny! What are 4, 2, 28 and 44?" Little Johnny quickly replied, "NBC, CBS, HBO, and the Cartoon Network!"

One night a wife found her husband standing over their baby's crib. Silently she watched him. As he stood looking down at the sleeping infant, she saw on his face a mixture of emotions, doubt, disbelief, delight, amazement, enchantment, skepticism. Touched by this unusual display and the deep emotions it aroused, with eyes glistening she slipped her arm around her husband." A penny for your thoughts," she said. "It's amazing!" he replied. "I just can't see how anybody can make a crib like that for only $46.50."

Texan bought a round of drinks for all in the bar and said that his wife had just produced "a typical Texas baby" weighing twenty pounds. From all a loud WOW and congratulations. Two weeks later he returned to the bar. The bartender recognized him and asked, "Aren't you the father of the typical Texas baby that weighed twenty pounds at birth? How much does he weigh now?" The proud father answered "10 pounds." The bartender said, "Why, what happened, he used to weigh twenty pounds?" The proud Texas father said "Just had him circumcised!"

A three-year-old boy went with his dad to see a new litter of kittens. On returning home, he breathlessly informed his mother, "There were two boy kittens and two girl kittens." "How did you know that?" his mother asked. "Daddy picked them up and looked underneath," he replied. "I think it's printed on the bottom."

Two women were walking down the street arguing. As they progressed the first woman turned to the second one and said "Let me be frank with you." The second woman replied "Bitch, you always think you get to be Frank!"

A little girl and a little boy were at day care one day. The girl approaches the boy and says, "Hey Tommy, wanna play house?" He says, "Sure. What do you want me to do?" The girl replies, "I want you to communicate," and he says to her, "That word is too big. I have no idea what it means." The little girl smirks and says, "Perfect. You can be the husband."

This little grandmother was surprised by her 7 year-old grandson one morning. He had made her coffee. She drank what was the worst cup of coffee in her life. When she got to the bottom there were those little green army men in the cup. She said, "Honey, what are these army men doing in my coffee?" Her grandson said, "Grandma, it says on TV- 'The best part of waking up is soldiers in your cup!"

When the mother returned from the grocery store, her small son pulled out the box of animal crackers he had begged for, then he spread the animal-shaped crackers all over the kitchen counter. "What are you doing?" his mom asked. "The box says you can't eat them if the seal is broken, so I'm looking for the seal."

I didn't know if my granddaughter had learned her colors yet, so I decided to test her. I would point out something and ask what color it was. She would tell me and always she was correct. But it was fun for me, so I continued. At last, she headed for the door, saying sagely, "Grandma, I think you should try to figure out some of these yourself!"

In the supermarket was a man pushing a cart which contained a screaming, bellowing baby. The gentleman kept repeating softly, "Don't get excited, Albert; don't scream, Albert; don't yell, Albert; keep calm, Albert." A woman standing next to him said "You certainly are to be commended for trying to soothe your son Albert." The man looked at her and said, "Lady, I'm Albert."

Differences between You & Your Boss

When you take a long time, you're slow.
When your boss takes a long time, he's thorough.

When you don't do it, you're lazy.
When your boss doesn't do it, he's too busy.

When you make a mistake, you're an idiot.
When your boss makes a mistake, he's only human.

When doing something without being told, you're overstepping your authority.
When your boss does the same thing that's initiative.

When you take a stand, you're being bull-headed.
When your boss does it, he's being firm.

When you overlooked a rule of etiquette, you're being rude.
When your boss skips a few rules, he's being original.

When you please your boss, you're apple polishing.
When your boss pleases his boss, he's being co-operative.

When you're out of the office, you're wandering around.
When your boss is out of the office, he's on business.

When you're on a day off sick, you're always sick.
When your boss is a day off sick, he must be very ill.

When you apply for leave, you must be going for an interview.
When your boss applies for leave, it's because he's overworked.

Q. How is a woman like a road?
A. Both have manholes.

One Sunday morning the pastor noticed little Johnny was standing staring up at the large plaque that hung in the foyer of the church. The young man of seven had been staring at the plaque for some time, so the pastor walked up and stood beside him and gazing up at the plaque he said quietly, "Good morning son.". "Good morning pastor" replied the young man not taking his eyes off the plaque. "Sir, what is this?" Johnny asked. "Well son, these are all the people who have died in the service," replied the pastor. Soberly, they stood together staring up at the large plaque. Little Johnny's voice barely broke the silence when he asked quietly, "Which one, sir, the 8:30 or the 10:30?"

Q. What's the difference between a mistress, a hooker and a wife?
A. The hooker says, "Faster, faster." The mistress says "Slower, slower." The wife says "Beige, I think we should paint the ceiling beige."

Man: Doctor, I can't stop singing "The Green, Green Grass Of Home". Can you help me?
Doctor: Ah yes, you appear to be suffering from Tom Jones Syndrome.
Man: Is it rare?

Doctor: Well, it’s not unusual.

It was a hot day in Minnesota. Helga hung the wash out to dry, put a roast in the oven, then went downtown to pick up some dry cleaning. “Gootness, it's hot,” she mused to herself as she walked down Main street. She passed by a tavern and thought, “Vy nodt?” so she walked in and took a seat at the bar. The bartender came up and asked her what she would like to drink. “Ya know,” Helga said, “it is so hot I tink I'll have myself zee cold beer.” The bartender asked, “Anheuser Busch?” Helga blushed and replied “Vell fine, tanks, und how's yer pecker?”

An 80 year old man is having his annual checkup. The doctor asks him how he's feeling “I've never been better!” he replies. “I've got an eighteen-year-old bride who's pregnant with my child! What do you think about that?” The doctor considers this for a moment, then says, “Well, let me tell you a story. I know a guy who's an avid hunter. He never misses a season. But one day he's in a bit of a hurry and he accidentally grabs his umbrella instead of his gun. So he's walking in the woods near a creek and suddenly spots a beaver in some brush in front of him! He raises up his umbrella, points it at the beaver and squeezes the handle. 'BAM' The beaver drops dead in front of him.” “That's impossible!” said the old man in disbelief. “Someone else must have shot that beaver.” “Exactly” said the Doctor.

The last four former U.S. Presidents are caught in a tornado, and off they spin to OZ. After a long walk down the yellow brick road, they finally make it to the Emerald City and come before the Great Wizard. “WHAT BRINGS YOU BEFORE THE GREAT WIZARD OF OZ? WHAT DO YOU WANT?” Jimmy Carter steps forward timidly: “I had a terrible time with Iran, so I've come for some courage”. “NO PROBLEM” says the Wizard, “WHO IS NEXT?” Ronald Reagan steps forward, “Well.., Well.., Well.., I need a brain.” “DONE” says the Wizard. “WHO COMES NEXT

BEFORE THE GREAT WIZARD?" Up steps George Bush sadly; "I'm told by the American people that I need a heart." "I'VE HEARD IT'S TRUE," says the Wizard. "CONSIDER IT DONE." Then there is a great silence. Bill Clinton is just standing there, looking around not saying a word. Irritated, the Wizard finally asks, "WELL, WHAT BRINGS YOU TO THE EMERALD CITY?" "Is Dorothy around?" Clinton replies.

Q. Why do all of the trees in Georgia point toward Atlanta?
A. Because Atlanta sucks!

Q. Why did Hitler commit suicide?
A. He got his gas bill.

Q. What is the difference between George W. Bush and Bill Clinton?
A. Bush keeps his Hummer in the garage.

Q. Why did the army send so many women with PMS to the Persian Gulf?
A. They fought like animals and retained water for 4 days.

A dedicated shop steward was at a convention in Las Vegas and decides to check out the local brothels. When he got to the first one, he asked the Madame, "Is this a union house?" "No, I'm sorry it isn't." "Well, if I pay you $100, what cut do the girls get?" "The house gets $80 and the girls get $20." Mightily offended at such unfair dealings, the man stomped off down the street in search of a more equitable shop. His search continued as long as you want to draw things out, until finally he reached a brothel where the Madame said, "Why yes, this is a union house." "And if I pay you $100, what cut do the girls get?" "The girls get $80 and the house gets $20." "That's more like it!" the man said. He looked around the room and pointed to a stunningly attractive redhead. "I'd like her for the night." "I'm sure you would, sir," said the Madame and gesturing to a fat fifty-year-old woman in the corner, "...but Bertha here has seniority!

A plane was taking off from Kennedy Airport. After it reached a comfortable cruising altitude, the captain made an announcement over the intercom, "Ladies and gentlemen, this is your captain speaking. Welcome to Flight Number 293, nonstop from New York to Los Angeles. The weather ahead is good and therefore we should have a smooth and uneventful flight. Now sit back and relax - OH MY GOD!" Silence followed and after a few minutes, the captain came back on the intercom and said, "Ladies and Gentlemen, I am so sorry if I scared you earlier, but while I was talking, the flight-attendant brought me a cup of coffee and spilled the hot coffee in my lap. You should see the front of my pants!" A passenger in Coach said, "That's nothing! He should see the BACK of mine!"

A large two-engine train was crossing America. After they had gone some distance, one of the engines broke down. "No problem," the engineer thought and carried on at half power. Farther on down the line, the other engine broke down and the train came to a standstill. The engineer decided he should inform the passengers about why the train had stopped, and made the following announcement, "Ladies and gentlemen, I have some good news and some bad news. The bad news is that both engines have failed, and we will be stuck here for some time. The good news is that you decided to take the train and not fly."

Q. What is a zebra?
A. 26 sizes larger than an "A" bra.

Q. How do you get holy water?
A. Boil the hell out of it.

Q. How does a spoiled rich girl change a light bulb?
A. She says, "Daddy, I want a new apartment."

One bright, beautiful Sunday morning, everyone in the tiny town got up early and went to the local church. Suddenly, Satan appeared at the front of the church. Everyone started screaming and running for the front entrance, trampling each other in frantic effort to get away from the evil one. Soon everyone was evacuated from the church, except for one elderly gentleman, who sat calmly in his pew, not moving, seemingly oblivious to the fact that God's ultimate enemy was in his presence. Now this confused Satan a bit, so he walked up to the man and said, "Don't you know who I am?" The man replied, "Yep, sure do." Satan asked, "Aren't you afraid of me?" "Nope, sure ain't" said the man. Satan was a little perturbed at this and queried, "Why aren't you afraid of me?" The man calmly replied, "Been married to your sister for over 48 years."

Q. What has four legs, is big, green, fuzzy, and if it fell out of a tree would kill you?
A. A pool table.

Q. What do prisoners use to call each other?
A. Cell phones.

Q. What do you call a boomerang that doesn't work?
A. A stick.

Q. What do you call cheese that isn't yours?
A. Nacho Cheese.

Q. What do you call four bull fighters in quicksand?
A. Quattro sinko.

Q. Why do gorillas have big nostrils?
A. Because they have big fingers.

The Americans and Russians at the height of the arms race realized that if they continued in the usual manner they were going to blow up the whole world. One day they sat down and decided to settle the whole dispute with one dog fight. They would have five years to breed the best fighting dog in the world and which ever side's dog won would be entitled to dominate the world. The Russians found the biggest meanest Doberman and Rottweiler female dogs in the world and bred them with the biggest meanest Siberian wolves. They selected only the biggest and strongest puppy from each litter, removed his siblings which gave him all the milk. After five years came up with the biggest meanest dog the world had ever seen. Its cage needed steel bars that were five inches thick and nobody could get near it. When the day came for the dog fight, the Americans showed up with a strange animal. It was a nine foot long Dachshund. Everyone felt sorry for the Americans because they knew there was no way that this dog could possibly last ten seconds with the Russian dog. When the cages were opened up, the Dachshund came out of its' cage and slowly waddled over towards the Russian dog. The Russian dog snarled and leaped out of its' cage and charged the American dachshund. But when it got close enough to bite the Dachshund's neck, the Dachshund opened its' mouth and consumed the Russian dog in one bite. There was nothing left of the Russian dog. The Russians came up to the Americans shaking their heads in disbelief. “We don't understand how this could have happened. We had our best people working for five years with the meanest Doberman and Rottweiler female dogs in the world and the biggest meanest Siberian wolves.” “That's nothing,” the American replied. “We had our best plastic surgeons working for five years to make an alligator look like a Dachshund.”

Q. Where do you get virgin wool from?
A. Ugly sheep.

A lecturer teaching medicine was tutoring a class on 'Observation'. He took out ajar of yellow-colored liquid. “This” he explained, “is urine. To be a doctor, you have to be observant to color, smell, sight, and taste.” After saying this, he dipped his finger into the jar and put it into his mouth. His class watched on in amazement, most, in disgust. But being the good students that they were, the jar was passed around and one by one, they dipped one finger into the jar then put it into their mouths. After the last student was done, the lecturer shook his head. "If any of you had been observant, you would have noticed that I put my 2nd finger into the jar and my 3rd finger into my mouth."

Q. What's black and blue and brown and laying in a ditch?
A. A brunette who's told too many blonde jokes.

Q. What do you call going on a blind date with a brunette?
A. Brown-bagging it.

Q. What's the real reason a brunette keeps her figure?
A. No one else wants it.

Q. What do you call a brunette in a room full of blondes?
A. Invisible.

Q. What's a brunette's mating call?
A. "Has the blonde left yet?"

Q. Why is the brunette considered an evil color?
A. When was the last time you saw a blonde witch?

Q. What do brunettes miss most about a great party?
A. The invitation

Q. What do you call a good looking man with a brunette?
A. A hostage

Q. Who makes bras for brunettes?
A. Fisher-Price

Q. Why are brunettes so proud of their hair?
A. It matches their mustache.

An English professor wrote the words, "a woman without her man is nothing" on the blackboard and directed the students to punctuate it correctly. The men wrote: "A woman, without her man, is nothing." The women wrote: "A woman: without her, man is nothing."

An Irishman arrived at J.F.K. Airport and wandered about the terminal with tears streaming down his cheeks. An airline employee asked him if he was already homesick. "No," replied the Irishman. "I've lost all me luggage!" "How'd that happen?" "The cork fell out" said the Irishman.

Three little boys were sitting on the porch, when one little boy says, "My Daddy smokes, and he can blow smoke rings." The second little boy pipes up, "Well, my Dad smokes too and can blow smoke out of his eyes." The third little boy, not to be outdone responds, "My Dad can blow smoke out of his butt." "Really, have you seen it?" reply the boys. The third boy responds, "No, but I've seen the tobacco stains on his underwear..."

On the first day of their Honeymoon, the very naive blond virgin bride slipped into a sexy but sweet nightie and, with great anticipation, crawled into bed, only to find that her new Christian husband had settled down on the couch. When she asked him why he was apparently not going to make love to her, he replied, "Because it's Lent." Almost in tears, she remarked "Well, that is the most ridiculous thing I have ever heard! To whom did you lend it, and for how long?"

A grizzled old man was eating in a truck stop when three Hell's Angels bikers walked in. The first biker approached the old man, threw his cigarette into the old man's pie, and then took seat at the counter. Then, a second biker walked over to the old man, spit into his glass of milk, and then took a seat at the counter. Finally, a third biker verbally attacked the old man, knocked his plate of food into his lap, and then took a seat at the counter. Without a word of protest, the old man quietly left the diner. Shortly thereafter, one of the bikers commented to the waitress, “Not much of a man is he?” The waitress replied, “Not much of a truck driver either, he just backed his truck over three motorcycles.”

A General retired after 35 years and realized a life-long dream of buying a bird-hunting estate in South Dakota. He invited an old friend to visit for a week of pheasant shooting. The friend was in awe of the General's new bird dog, “Sarge”. The dog could point, flush and retrieve with the very best, and the friend offered to buy the dog at any price. The General declined, saying that Sarge was the very best bird dog he had ever owned and that he wouldn't part with him at any price. A year later the same friend returned for another week of hunting and was surprised to find the General breaking in a new dog. “What happened to ole Sarge” he asked? “Had to shoot him” grumbled the General. “A friend came to hunt with me and couldn't remember the dog's name. He kept calling him Colonel. After that, all he would do was sit on his ass and bark.”

This woman has her bridge club every Thursday night and after a peaceful game or two with the ladies, she goes home to fix her husband dinner when he gets home from work. Well, one Thursday, she's playing a great game and she has an incredible hand when she notices the time. “Oh no, I have to go fix my husband his dinner! He's going to be so angry if it's not ready on time” and she dashes out of her friend's house, her great hand forgotten on the table. When she gets home, she realizes she does not enough time to go to the supermarket and all she has in the kitchen is a wilted lettuce leaf, an egg, and a can of cat food. In a panic, she opens the can of cat food, stirs in the egg, and garnishes it with the lettuce leaf just as her husband is pulling up in the driveway. She watches in anticipation as he sits down to his dinner, and then she realizes he is loving it! "Mmmm, this is the best dinner you've made for me in forty years of marriage. You can make this for me any old day, mmmm!" That night they had sex for the first time in months and it was great! Needless to say, every Thursday from then on she made this dinner for her husband. She tells her bridge cronies about it and they're all horrified. "You're going to kill him," they say, or "He's just yanking your chain," but she continued to make him his cat food dinner and then, afterwards, they would bonk like fiends. Two months later, her husband died and the Thursday after the funeral, all the bridge women attacked our new widow for being so callous. "You killed him! We told you that feeding him that cat food every week would do him in! How can you just sit there so calmly and play bridge knowing you murdered your husband?" The wife stoically replied, "Oh I didn't kill him he fell off the mantel when he was licking his ass."

In the restroom at work, the Boss had placed a sign directly above the sink. It had a single word on it "Think!" The next day, when he went to the restroom, he looked at the sign and right below it immediately above the soap dispenser, someone had carefully lettered another sign which read "Thoap!"

SOME SIGNS THAT YOU'RE OLD

You get up to change the TV channel and decide as long as you're up, you might as well go to bed.

In the morning you hear snap, crackle, pop, and it isn't your breakfast cereal.

You start complaining that "They're building car seats too low!"

Your ears perk up when a laxative commercial comes on TV.

You call the place you keep leftovers the "icebox."

You wonder why everyone is starting to mumble.

You start videotaping daytime game shows.

When you do the hokey pokey and you "put your left hip out" ... it stays out.

One of the throw pillows on your bed is a hot-water bottle.

Your underwear starts creeping up on you ... and you enjoy it.

You worry because you don't have any symptoms

You spend more time on the menu than the waitress

Your keyboard cable is still kinky and you're not

You feel your corns more than you do your oats

Your actions creak louder than your words

You wake up in the middle of the night tired and listless

You know "where it's at", but forgot why it's there

You know how to spell gastroenterologist

Your biological urges are more like occasional nudges

You have to attend porno flicks with an interpreter

You don't have any enemies because you've outlived them all

You don't date women your own age, because there aren't any

You have to use tenderizer to eat all your cream of soups

"Happy Hour" now consists of a nap

You remember what you did yesterday by what hurts today

Everything that works hurts, and what doesn't hurt doesn't work.

You feel like the morning after, and you haven't been anywhere.

Your little black book only contains names ending in M.D.

Your children are beginning to look middle-aged.

Your mind makes contracts your body can't keep.

You look forward to a dull evening.

Your knees buckle and your belt won't.

Your back goes out more than you do.

You sink your teeth into a steak, and they stay there.

You know all the answers, but nobody asks the questions.

A depressed young woman was so desperate that she decided to end her life by throwing herself into the ocean. When she went down to the docks, a handsome young sailor noticed her tears, took pity on her, and said, "Look, you've got a lot to live for. I'm off to Europe in the morning, and if you like, I can stow you away on my ship. I'll take good care of you and bring you food every day." Moving closer, he slipped his arm around her shoulder and added, "I'll keep you happy, and you'll keep me happy." The girl nodded yes, after all, what did she have to lose? That night, the sailor brought her aboard and hid her in a life-boat. From then on, every night he brought her three sandwiches and a piece of fruit, and they made passionate love until dawn. Three weeks later, during a routine search, she was discovered by the captain. "What are you doing here?" the Captain asked. "I have an arrangement with one of the sailors," she explained. "He's taking me to Europe, and he's screwing me." "He sure is lady... this is the Staten Island Ferry!"

One day, while God was looking into the Garden of Eden, he noticed Eve skinny-dipping in the river. "Damn!! I'll NEVER be able to get THAT smell out of the fish!!"

What's in a name?

A number of years ago there was a proposed merger between Fairchild Electronics and Honeywell Computers. Rumor had it that the new company would be called Fairwell Honeychild.

There is a merger in the works involving Polygraph Records, Warner Brothers and Keebler. It will be called Poly-Warner-Cracker.

There has long been a rumor that W. R. Grace Co. was going to buy the Fuller Brush Co. and Mary Kay Cosmetics and then merge with the Hale Business Systems. This would result in the new mega-corporation Hale Mary Fuller Grace.

Don't forget the failed merger between Yahoo and Netscape: Net'n'Yahoo. It didn't work out because they were afraid they would have to relocate the headquarters to Tel Avi.

3M & Goodyear = MMMGood

Honeywell & Imasco & Home Oil = Honey, I'm Home

Knott's Berry Farm & National Organization Of Women = Knott NOW

Zippo & Audi & Dofasco / Dakota Mining - Zip Audi DoDa

A city slicker moves to the country and decides he's going to take up farming. He heads to the local co-op and tells the man, “Give me 100 baby chickens.” The co-op man complies. A week later the man returns and says. Give me 300 baby chickens.” The co-op man complies. Again, a week later the man returns. This time he says, “Give me 500 baby chickens.” “Wow!” the co-op man replies. “You must really be doing well!” “Naw” said the man with a sigh “I'm either planting them too deep or too far apart!”

<u>Some things men can say when getting caught looking at another woman:</u>
I think that's a man dressed as woman.

Isn't that the actress from the movie Delicatessen (chances are she hasn't seen that movie - and neither have you but you will get brownie points naming a foreign film, and it will be just obtuse enough to distract her).

I think that's the girl I knew from high school who eventually joined a convent (or was committed to an asylum) and turned out to be a real nut case.

I was just thinking how I felt sorry for her, since she can't hold a candle to you (this one might not work but it's worth a try).

“Do you think she's prettier than me?” Give her a taste of her own medicine.

I got something in my eye... can't see a thing!

That's the loser I dumped in order to go out with you. Boy, am I glad I got away from her. What a moron.

I know you're probably thinking I was staring at a beautiful woman, but to me she is like one of those fancy bakery cakes that looks good, but then you have a bite and it is so sweet that it makes you sick. She makes me sick. (It helps if you convulse a little).

One sunny afternoon, a bored Superman was out flying around. Crime was slow that day, so he decided to go over to Spiderman's house. "Hey Spidey, let's go get a burger and a beer!" "No can do, Supe. I've got a problem with my web shooter. Can't fight crime without it!" So, Superman heads over to the Bat Cave to see what Batman was up to. "Hey Batman, let's go get a burger and a beer!" "Not today my friend. My Batmobile is down and it must be fixed today. Can't fight crime tomorrow without it." Disgruntled, Superman takes to the air. Cruising around the skies, he flies over a penthouse apartment and with his Super Vision what does he see? None other than a naked Wonder Woman on the bed, laying spread eagle and stark-naked. Superman gets a brilliant idea thinking, he's faster than a speeding bullet and always wondered what it would be like with her Wonder Powers. So he zooms down, does her in a flash and is gone before she can notice. All of a sudden, Wonder Woman sits up and says "What was that?" The Invisible Man gets off her and replies "I don't know, but my ass hurts like hell."

<u>Things To Say If You Get Caught Sleeping At Your Desk</u>

15. "They told me at the blood bank this might happen."
14. "This is just a 15 minute power-nap like they raved about in the last time management course you sent me to."
13. "Whew! Guess I left the top off the liquid paper."
12. "I wasn't sleeping! I was meditating on the mission statement and envisioning a new paradigm."

11. "This is one of the seven habits of highly effective people."
10. "I was testing the keyboard for drool resistance."
9. "Actually I'm doing a "Stress Level Elimination Exercise Plan" (SLEEP) I learned it at the last mandatory seminar you made me attend."
8. "I was doing a highly specific Yoga exercise to relieve work related stress."
7. "Darn! Why did you interrupt me? I had almost figured Out a solution to the biggest problem."
6. "The coffee machine is broken...."
5. "Someone must've put decaf in the coffee pot."
4. "Boy, that cold medicine I took last night just won't wear off!"
3. "Ah, the unique and unpredictable circadian rhythms of the workaholic!"
2. "I wasn't sleeping I was trying to pick up my contact lens without any hands"
1. "Amen."

It was George the mailman's last day on the job after 35 years of carrying the mail through all kinds of weather to the same neighborhood. When he arrived at the first house on his route he was greeted by the whole family there who roundly and soundly congratulated him and sent him on his way with a gift envelope. At the second house they presented him with a box of fine cigars. The folks at the third house handed him a selection of ten fishing lures. At the fourth house he was met at the door by a strikingly beautiful woman in a revealing negligee. She took him by the hand, gently led him through the door (which she closed behind him), and led him up the stairs to the bedroom where she blew his mind with the most passionate love making he had ever experienced. When he had had enough they went downstairs, where she fixed him a giant breakfast: eggs, potatoes, ham, sausage, blueberry pancakes and fresh-squeezed orange juice. When he was truly satisfied she poured him a cup of steaming coffee. As she was pouring he noticed a dollar bill sticking out from under the cups bottom. This was just too wonderful for words. He said, "What's the dollar for?" "Well," she said "last night, I told my husband that today would be your last day and that he should do something special for you. I asked him what to give you and he said "Screw him, give him a dollar." The breakfast was my idea.

Marine Colonel on his way home from work at the Pentagon came to a dead halt in traffic and thought to himself, "Wow, this traffic seems worse than usual. Nothing's even moving." He notices a police officer walking back and forth between the lines of cars so he rolls down his window and asks, "Excuse me, Officer, what's the holdup? The Officer replies, "The President is just so depressed about his low approval ratings he stopped his motorcade in the middle of the Beltway and he's threatening to douse himself in gasoline and set himself on fire. He says his family hates him and he doesn't have the money for his healthcare plan. I'm walking round taking up a collection for him." The Colonel asks "How much have you collected so far?" The Officer replies, "So far only about 310 gallons of gas but I've got a lot of folks still siphoning."

A pretty blonde woman is driving down a country road in her new sports car when something goes wrong and it breaks down. Luckily she happens to be near a farmhouse. She goes up to the farmhouse and knocks on the door. When the farmer answers, she says to him "It's Sunday night and my car broke down and I don't know what to do! Can I stay here for the night until tomorrow when I can get some help?" "Well," drawls the farmer, "you can stay here, but I don't want you messin' with my sons Jed and Luke." She looks through the screen door and sees two men standing behind the farmer. She judges them to be in the early twenties. "Okay," she says. After they have gone to bed for the night the woman begins to get a little horny just thinking about the two boys in the room next to her. So she quietly goes into their room and says, "Boys, how would you like for me to teach you the ways of the world?" They say, "Yeah?" She says, "The only thing is, I don't want to get pregnant so you have to wear these rubbers." She puts them on the boys and the three of the go it all night long. Forty years later, Jed and Luke were sitting on the front porch, rocking back and forth. Jed says "Luke, you remember that blond woman that came by here about 40 years ago and showed us the ways of the world?" "Yeah" says Luke "I remember." "Well, do you care if she gets pregnant" asks Jed. "Nope," says Luke, "I reckon not." "Me neither" says Jed, "let's take these things off."

Three men were standing in line to get into heaven one day. Apparently it had been a pretty busy day, though, so Peter had to tell the first one, "Heaven's getting pretty close to full today, and I've been asked to admit only people who have had particularly horrible deaths. So what's your story'?" So the first man replies: "Well, for a while I've suspected my wife has been cheating on me, so today I came home early to try to catch her red-handed. As I came into my 25th floor apartment, I could tell something was wrong, but all my searching around didn't reveal where this other guy could have been hiding. Finally, I went out to the balcony and sure enough, there was this man hanging off the railing 25 floors above ground. By now I was really mad, so I started beating on him and kicking him. Of course, he couldn't stand that for long, so he let go and fell but he landed in the bushes, stunned but alive. I couldn't stand it anymore, so I ran into the kitchen, grabbed the fridge and threw it over the edge. It landed on him killing him instantly. But, all the stress and anger got to me, and I had a heart attack and died there on the balcony." "That sounds like a pretty bad day to me," said Peter, and let the man in. The second man comes up, Peter explains to him about Heaven being full and again asks for his story. "It's been a very strange day. You see, I live on the 26th floor of an apartment building, and every morning I do my exercises out on my balcony. Well, this morning I must have slipped or something because I fell over the edge. But I got lucky, and caught tile railing of the balcony on the floor below me. I knew I couldn't hang on for very long, when suddenly this man burst out onto the balcony. I thought for sure I was saved, when all of a sudden he started beating on me and kicking me. I held on the best I could, but he ran into the apartment, grabbed a hammer and started pounding on my hands. Finally, I let go. But again, I got lucky and fell into the bushes below, stunned but all right. Just when I was thinking I was going to be okay, this refrigerator comes falling out of the sky and crushes me instantly, and now I'm here." Once again Peter had to concede that that sounded like a pretty horrible death and let him into Heaven. The third man came to the front of the line, and again the whole process was repeated as Peter explained that Heaven was full and asked for his story. "Picture this," says the third man, "I'm hiding naked inside a refrigerator..."

The Queen was visiting one of Canada's hospitals, and during her tour of the floors she passed a room where a male patient was masturbating. "Oh my," said the Queen, "what's going on there?" The Doctor who was taking her around on the tour explained "That man's testicles rapidly fill with semen and if he doesn't do that 7 times a day they will explode." "Oh, my!" said the Queen. On the next floor they passed a room where a young nurse was giving a patient a blow job. "Oh", said the Queen, "what's going on in there?" The Doctor replied, "Same problem but better health plan."

A Frenchman, an Italian and a Texan were discussing love making. "Last night I made love to my wife three times" boasted the Frenchman. "She was in sheer ecstasy this morning." "Ah, last night, I made love to my wife six times" the Italian responded, "and this morning she made me a wonderful omelet and told me she could never love another man." When the Texan remained silent, the Frenchman smugly asked. "And how many times did you make love to your wife last night?" "Once" he replied. "Only once?" the Italian arrogantly snorted. "And what did she say to you this morning?" "Don't stop!!!"

Before And After You Fall In Love:

Before- You take my breath away
After- I feel like I'm suffocating.

B- Twice a night.
A- Twice a month.

B- She says she loves the way I take control of a situation.
A- She called me a controlling, manipulative, egomaniac.

B- Lucy and Ricky.
A-Fred and Ethyl.

B- Saturday night fever.
A- Monday night football.

B- He makes me feel like a million dollars.
A- If I had a dime for every stupid thing he's done.

B- Don't stop.
A- Don't start.

B- The sound of music.
A- The sounds of silence.

B- Is that all you're having?
A- Maybe you should have just a salad honey.

B- Wheel of Fortune.
A- Jeopardy.

B- It's like I'm living in a dream.
A- It's like he lives in a dorm.

B- $60/dozen.
A- $1.50/stem.

B- Turbo charged.
A- Jump start.

B- We agree on everything.
A- Doesn't she have a mind of her own?

B- Victoria's Secret.
A- Fruit of the Loom.

B- Charming and noble.
A- Chernobyl.

B- Feathers and handcuffs.
A- Ball and chain.

B- I love a woman with curves.
A- I never said you were fat.

B- He's completely lost without me.
A- Why won't he ever ask for directions?

B- Time stood still.
A- This relationship is going nowhere.

B- Croissant and cappuccino.
A- Bagel and instant.

B- Blind.
A- Nearsighted.

B- You look so seductive in black.
A- Your clothes are so depressing.

B- Oysters.
A- Fish sticks.

B- I can hardly believe we found each other.
A- I can't believe I ended up with someone like you.

B- Passion.
A- Ration.

B- Once upon a time.
A- The end.

How many animals can fit into one pair of pantyhose?
10 little piggy's, 2 calves, an ass, a beaver and a fish that no one can seem to find.

The manager of a large office noticed a new man one day and asked him to come to his office. What is your name was the first thing the manager asked the new guy. John the guy replied. The manager scowled, “Look, I don't know what kind of a namby-pamby place you worked at before, but I don't call anyone by their first name. It breeds familiarity and that leads to a breakdown in authority. I refer to my employees by their last name only Smith, Jones, Baker that's all. I am to be referred to only as Mr. Robertson. Now that we got that straight, what is your last name?” The new guy sighed and said. “Darling. My name is John Darling.” “Okay, John, the next thing I want to tell you is...”

<u>Inventions by Blondes</u>
-- The water-proof towel
-- Glow in the dark sunglasses
-- Solar powered flashlights
-- Submarine screen doors
-- A book on how to read
-- Inflatable dart boards
-- A dictionary index
-- Mechanical Pencil sharpeners
-- Powdered water
-- Pedal-powered wheel chairs
-- Waterproof tea bags

-- Zero proof alcohol
-- Re-useable ice cubes
-- See-through toilet tissue
-- Skinless bananas
-- Do-it-yourself road map
-- Turnip ice cream
-- Toe implants
-- An all white flag
-- Rolls Royce pickup truck

A rabbi had a terrible car wreck and was rushed to a local Catholic hospital. After the doctors patched him up, he recuperated in the orthopedic ward for several weeks. As he recovered from his injuries he became friends with the Sister who was a nurse there. One day, she came into his room and noticed that the crucifix on the wall was missing. She asked him good-naturedly, “Rabbi, what have you done with the crucifix?” “Sister” chuckled the rabbi, “I just figured one suffering Jew in this room was enough.”

A guy goes to the tattoo parlor and offers the tattoo artist $1,000 to put a $100 bill on his willie. The artist agrees but is curious and asks the man why he wants to do this. The man replies “I have my reasons which I would rather not tell right now.” So, the artist goes ahead and does the job all the while he is anxious with curiosity over why this man wants a $100 bill tattooed on his penis. So he tells the man that he really needs to know the reason. He tells the man he can keep his $1000 if he would just tell him the reason for putting a tattoo of a $100 bill on his willie. The man consents and offers these three reasons: “First, I like to play with my money. Second, I like to watch my money grow. And third, and most importantly, the next time my wife wants to blow $100, she can stay home to do it!”

A guy walks into a post office one day to see a middle aged, balding man standing at the counter methodically placing “Love” stamps on bright pink envelopes with hearts all over them. He then takes out a perfume bottle and starts spraying the scent all over them. His curiosity got the better him, so he goes up to the balding man and asks him what he is doing. The man says "I'm sending out 1000 Valentine cards signed, 'Guess who'?" "But why?" asks the man. "I'm a divorce lawyer" the man replies.

A man and a woman are standing at a cocktail party when the woman remarks, "You know, you look just like my third husband." "How many times have you been married?" asks the man. "Twice" replies the lady.

A man who says marriage is a 50/50 proposition doesn't understand two things: first women and second fractions.

Why does a woman work ten years to change a man's habits and then complain that he's not the same man she married?

Charlie, a door-to-door vacuum cleaner salesman goes to the first house in his new territory. He knocks on the door and a real mean, tough looking lady opens the door. Before she has a chance to say anything, he runs inside and dumps cow patties all over the carpet. Charlie says, "Lady, if this vacuum cleaner can't clean up that cow manure, I'll eat a shit sandwich." The tough lady smirks and says "Okay, but do you want ketchup on that shit sandwich?" The salesman says "Why do you ask, my vacuum is the strongest cleaner around?" She says "We just moved in and we haven't got the electricity turned on yet."

Why don't police cars have a bumper sticker that says "How's my driving?"

What do the Vacuum "Dirt Devil" and Viagra have in common?
They both put the power of an upright in the palm of your hand.

AMNESIA: The condition that enables a woman who has gone through labor to have sex again.

Patient: "Doctor, my wife thinks I'm crazy because I like sausages."
Psychiatrist: "Nonsense! I like sausages too."
Patient: "Good, you should come see my collection. I've got hundreds of them."

I hate to repeat gossip, so I'll only say this once.

I don't eat snails... I prefer FAST food!

I don't think, therefore I am not.

Q: How can you tell if you are in a gay church?
A: Only half of the congregation is kneeling!

Bob was driving home and topped a hill at about 90 mph. Wouldn't you know it, a cop jumped out and clocked him with radar. Bob pulled over like a good citizen, recalling Rodney King and recent illegal alien incidents. The cop walked up to the window and said. "You know how fast you were going, BOY?" Bob thought for a second and asked, "Uh...over fifty-five". "93 mph, son, 93 mph in a 55 zone!" said the cop. "But if you already knew officer" replied Bob, "why did you ask me?" Ignoring Bob, the officer continued in his normal, charming fashion. "That's speeding so you're getting a ticket and a fine!" The cop took a good look at Bob and said. "You don't even look like you have a job! Why, I've never seen anyone so cruddy in my entire life!" Bob answered, "I've got a job. I have a good paying job!" The cop leaned in the window and with the smell of old donuts on his breath said, "What kind of a job could a bum like you have?" "I'm a rectum stretcher!" replied Bob. "What did you say BOY" asked patrolman. "I'm a rectum stretcher!" Of course, the cop asked "What does a rectum stretcher do?" Bob explained, "People call me up and say they want to be stretched, so I go over there and start with a couple of fingers, then a couple more, and then one whole hand. Then two hands. Then I pull them farther and farther apart until it's six feet across." The cop, absorbed with the images in his mind, let down his guard and asked, "What the hell do you do with a six foot asshole?" Bob nonchalantly commented, "You give it a radar gun and stick it at the top of a hill."

After being with his blind date all evening, the man couldn't take another minute with her. Earlier, he had secretly arranged to have a friend call him on the restaurant phone so he would have an excuse to leave if something like this happened. When he returned to the table, he lowered his eyes, put on a grim expression and said, "I have some bad news. My grandfather just died." "Thank heavens" his date replied "I thought mine would have had to die!"

This guy has four daughters and one Friday night the doorbell rings. The guy answers it and a kid standing there says "Hi, I'm Freddy. I'm here to pick up Betty. We're gonna go eat spaghetti. Is she ready?" "The man, mildly amused calls down his daughter and they leave. A few minutes later the doorbell rings again and he answers. A kid standing there says "Hi, I'm Jim. I'm here to see Kim. We're gonna go for a swim. Can I come in?" The guy, now perplexed, says "Yes." and the two take off. A few minutes later the doorbell rings and again the father answers. A kid standing there says "Hi, I'm Joe. I'm here to pick up Flo. We're gonna go to the show. Can she go?" The man, now annoyed, says "Yes" and the two depart. Sure enough, the door rings and the father answers it again. A kid standing there says "Hi. I'm Chuck…" The father shot him.

A man and woman were having dinner in a restaurant. Their waitress who was a few paces away, suddenly notices that the man was slowly sliding down his chair and under the table. His date acted unconcerned. The waitress watched as the man slid all the way down his chair and out of sight under the table. The woman dining across from him still appeared calm, apparently unaware that her dining companion had disappeared. Concerned, the waitress came over to the table and said to the woman “Pardon me ma'am, but I think your husband just slid under the table.” The woman calmly looked up at her and replied firmly “No he didn't, my husband just walked in the door.”

An old cowboy, dressed to kill, with his best cowboy hat and shirt, jeans, spurs, chaps, boots and belt buckle, went to a bar and ordered a drink. While he sat sipping his whiskey, a young lady sat down next to him. She ordered a drink, turned to the cowboy and asked “Are you a cowboy?” “Well,” he began “I have spent my whole life on the ranch, herding cows, breaking horses, mending fences, so I guess I am. What about you?” “I've never been on a ranch” she said “so I'm not a cowboy, but I am a lesbian.” “What's a lesbian?” asked the cowboy who obviously had been out on the ranch too long. “Let’s just say that I spend my whole day thinking about women” she replied. “As soon as I get up in the morning I think of women. Whether I eat, shower or watch television, everything seems to make me think about women.” After a while, she left the bar and the cowboy ordered another whiskey. A young couple sat down next to him and asked “Are you a real cowboy?” I always thought I was” he replied “but I just found out that I am a lesbian.”

Two priests died at the same time and met St. Peter at the Pearly Gates. St. Peter said “I'd like to take you guys in now, but our computer is down so you'll have to go back to Earth for about a week. However, you can't go back as priests, so what else would you like to be” The first priest says “I've always wanted to be an eagle, soaring above the Rocky Mountains.” “So be it” says St. Peter and off flies the first priest. The second priest mulls this over for a moment and asks “Will any of this week ‘Count’?” St. Peter said “No, I told you the computer's down. There's no way we can keep track of what you're doing.” “In that case” says the second priest, “I've always wanted to be a stud.” “So be it” says St. Peter, and the second priest disappears. A week goes by, the computer is fixed, and the Lord tells St. Peter to recall the two priests. “Will you have any trouble locating them?” God asks. “The first one should he easy” says St. Peter. “He's somewhere over the Rockies, flying with the eagles. But the second one could prove to be a bit more difficult.” “Why?” asked the Lord. “Well, he's on a snow tire, somewhere in North Dakota.”

Bill and Hillary are out driving in the country near Hillary's hometown. They are low on fuel, so Bill pulls into a gas station for a fill-up. The attendant comes out and starts to pump gas into the former first couple's tank. As he is doing this, he looks into the passenger window and says “Hey, Hillary, we used to date in high school, do you remember me?” he asks. They chat for a few minutes, Bill pays and the First couple leaves. As they off drive Bill looks over at Hillary and says “You used to date that guy? Just think what it would be like if you had married him” he says smugly. Hillary looks at Bill, shrugs her shoulders and replies “Well I guess you'd be pumping gas and he would be the President.”

Yesterday scientists revealed that beer contains small traces of female hormones. To test their theory the scientists fed 100 men 10 pints of beer and observed that 100% of them gained weight, talked excessively without making sense became emotional, couldn't drive, couldn't think and refused to apologize when wrong. No further testing is planned.

Famous Last Words!
I'll get a world record for this.

Let me reach in and get your watch out of the printing press.

Hey there's no handles inside these car doors!

Gee, that's a cute tattoo.

Let's ask that group of basketball players for directions.

Here's my Kent State student ID.

It's fireproof.

He's probably just hibernating.

What does this button do?

I'm making a citizen's arrest.

Can we get a vision plan?

So, you're a cannibal.

It's probably just a rash.

Why am I standing on a plastic sheet?

Are you sure the power is off?

Yeah, I made the deciding vote on the jury, SO what of it?

No, my shoes aren't untied.

The odds of that happening have to be a million to one!

What duck?

What do you mean “I'll be back”.

Pull the pin and count to what?

Which wire was I supposed to cut?

I wonder where the mother bear is.

I've seen this done on TV.

These are the good kind of mushrooms.

I'll hold it and you light the fuse.

What's that priest doing here?

You look just like Charles Manson.

Let it down slowly.

Rat poison only kills rats.

I hope they speak English.

OK…I'll go ahead and make your day.

It can't possibly rain for forty days and nights.

I'll get your toast out.

Give me liberty or give me death.

Just take whatever you want, this is a ghost town.

It's strong enough for both of us.

That birthmark on your head looks like 999.

This doesn't taste right.

I can make this light before it changes.

Nice doggie.

I can do that with my eyes closed.

I've done this before.

Well, we've made it this far.

That's odd.

Hey, that's not a violin.

I'll just slip into the commuter lane for a second.

I don't think we're in Kansas anymore.

You wouldn't hit a guy with glasses would you?

OK, this is the last time.

Don't be so superstitious.

Now watch this.

This planet has an atmosphere just like on earth.

A building contractor was being paid by the week for a job that was likely to stretch over several months. He approached the owner of the property and held up the check he'd been given. "This is two hundred dollars less than we agreed on" he said. "I know," the owner said "but last week I overpaid you two hundred dollars, and you never complained." The contractor said "Well, I don't mind an occasional mistake but when it gets to be a habit, I feel I have to call it to your attention."

You know your life stinks when….
A black cat crosses your path and it drops dead.

You take an assertiveness training course and you're afraid

to tell your wife.

The candles on your cake set off the smoke alarm.

Your chauffer is on parole for car theft.

You have to take out a loan just to get money for a down payment.

Your children's school calls to surrender.

The bride's family throws rocks instead of rice.

Your wife wraps your lunch in a road map.

Your plants do better when you don't talk to them.

All your modeling jobs are for cartoonists.

Your engagement ring, upon closer inspection, is plastic.

The following phrase: PRESIDENT CLINTON OF THE USA can be rearranged (with no letters left over, and using each letter only once) into: TO COPULATE HE FINDS INTERNS.

As a painless way to save money, a young couple arranged that every time they have sex, the husband puts his pocket change into a china piggy bank on the bedside table. One night while being unusually athletic, he accidentally knocked the bank to the floor where it smashes to pieces. To his surprise, among the masses of coins, there are handfuls of five and ten dollar bills. He asks his wife, "What's up with all of those big bills in here?" "Well," she replied "Not everyone is as cheap as you are…."

Q. What do you get when you cross Monica Lewinsky with Unabomber Ted Kaczynski?
A. A dynamite blowjob.

A guy is nearing the end of his senior year in high school but he still has to share a room with his younger brother, who is only 9 years old. One night he decides to bring his girlfriend over for a little fun. There are bunk beds and the guy notices that his little brother is already asleep on the lower bunk, so he and his girlfriend climb up to the top one. As you might expect things start to heat up. He remembers that his little brother is sleeping below them so he tells his girlfriend to whisper “lettuce” if she wants it harder and “tomato” if she wants a new position. “Lettuce! Tomato! Lettuce!! Tomato!! Lettuce!!! Tomato!!!” she screams. “Lettuce!!!!! Tomato!!!! Whoa, PULL IT OUT…PULL IT OUT NOW…I can't get pregnant!” Then the little brother shouts up “Hey, would you guys stop making sandwiches up there, you're getting mayonnaise all over my face!”

The teacher in Johnny's school asked the class what their parents did for a living. One little girl said her father was a doctor, another said her mother was an engineer. When it was Little Johnny's turn, he stood up and said “My mom's a whore.” Naturally after that remark, he got sent off to the principal's office. 15 minutes later, he returned to class, so the teacher asked “Did you tell the principal what you said in class?” Johnny answered “Yes, I did.” “Well, what did the principal have to say.” “He said that every job is important, gave me an apple and asked for her phone number.”

A man walks into a Porsche dealership, opened the door of a red Boxster, took a seat behind the wheel and smiled. A salesman approached and asked, “Are you thinking about buying this car?” “Nope,” he said, “but I am thinking about all the pussy I could get if I owned it.”

Q. What does Monica Lewinsky and a Coke machine have in common?

A. They both have a slot that says “Insert Bill Here”.

An actual question given for mid-term chemistry exam at University of Washington: “Is Hell exothermic (radiates heat) or endothermic (absorbs heat)? Support your answer with a proof.” Most of the students wrote proofs of their beliefs using Boyle's Law (gas cools when it expands and heats up when it is compressed) or some variant. One student, however, wrote the following: “First, we need to know how the mass of Hell is changing in time. So we need to know the rate that souls are moving into Hell and the rate they are leaving. I think that we can safely assume that once a soul gets to Hell, it will not leave, therefore, no souls are leaving. As for how many souls are entering Hell, let's look at the different religions that exist in the world today. Some of these religions state that if you are not a member of their religion that you will go to Hell. Since there are more than one of these types of religions and since people do not belong to more than one religion at a time, we can project that all people and therefore all souls will go to Hell. With birth and death rates as they are, we can expect the number of souls in Hell to increase exponentially. Now we look at the rate of change of the Volume in Hell, because Boyle's Law states that in order for the temperature and pressure in Hell to stay the same, the volume of Hell has to expand as souls are added. This gives two possibilities: (1) If Hell is expanding at a slower rate than the rate at which souls enter Hell, then the temperature and pressure in Hell will increase until all Hell breaks loose. (2) Hell is expanding at a rate faster than the increase of souls so the temperature and pressure will drop until Hell freezes over. So which is correct? If we accept the postulate given to me by Miss Therese Banyan during my Freshman year that “it will be a cold day in Hell before I sleep with you” and given the fact that I still have not succeeded in having sexual relations with her, then (2) cannot be true. Therefore, Hell is exothermic.” The student got the only “A” in the class.

If we are what we eat then I'm fast, easy and cheap.

If a messy kitchen is a happy kitchen, then my kitchen must be delirious!

A balanced diet is having a cookie in each hand.

Thou shall not weigh more than thy refrigerator.

A clean kitchen is a sign of frozen food.

Help keep our kitchen clean, eat out a lot.

THE RULES OF CHOCOLATE

If you've got melted chocolate all over your hands, you're eating it much too slowly.

Chocolate covered raisins, cherries, orange slices and strawberries all count as fruit, so eat as many as you want.

The problem: How to get 2 pounds of chocolate home from the store in hot car.
The solution: Eat it in the parking lot.

Diet tip: Eat a chocolate bar before each meal because it'll take the edge off your appetite and you'll eat less.

A nice box of chocolates can provide your total daily intake of calories all in one place. Isn't that handy?

If calories are an issue, store your chocolate on top of the fridge.
Calories are afraid of heights and they might jump out of the chocolate to protect themselves.

If I eat equal amounts of dark chocolate and white chocolate is that a balanced diet? Don't they actually counteract each other?
Money talks but chocolate sings.

Q. Why is there no such organization as Chocoholics Anonymous?
A. Simple, no one wants to quit.

If not for chocolate, there would be no need for control top pantyhose. An entire garment industry would be devastated.

Put "eat chocolate" at the top of your list of things to do today.

Ten Things Not To Do In The Nude

10. Fry bacon.
9. Arc weld.
8. Bathe a cat.
7. Operate a snow blower.
6. Clear a patch of poison ivy.
5. Insulate the attic with fiberglass.
4. Operate a lathe.
3. Present a children's television show.
2. Take Mass with the Pope.

And the number 1 thing not to do in the nude: Pick up a dime from a San Francisco sidewalk.

I got a set of golf clubs for my husband, and I must say, "It was a damn good trade".

A married man and his secretary were having a torrid affair. One afternoon they couldn't contain their passion, so they rushed over to her place where they spent the afternoon making passionate love. When they were finished, they fell asleep and didn't wake up until 8 o'clock. They got dressed quickly then the man told his secretary to take his shoes outside and rub them on the lawn. She is bewildered but does as he asks. The man finally gets home and his wife meets him at the door. Upset, she asks where he's been. The man replies "I cannot tell a lie, my secretary and I are having an affair. Today we left work early, went to her place, spent the afternoon making love then fell asleep. That's why I'm late."

"The wife looks at him, takes notice of his shoes and says "I see those are grass stains on your shoes. YOU GODDAMN LIAR!!! You've been playing golf again, haven't you?"

TOP TEN THINGS ONLY WOMEN UNDERSTAND

10. Cats/dogs facial expressions.
9. The need for the same style of shoes in different colors.
8. Why bean sprouts aren't just weeds.
7. Fat clothes.
6. Taking a car trip without trying to beat your best time.
5. The difference between beige, off-white, and eggshell.
4. Cutting your bangs to make them grow.
3. Eyelash curlers.
2. The inaccuracy of every bathroom scale ever made.

And the Number One thing: *OTHER WOMEN.*

An elderly Mr. Steinberg and the widow Joyce Cohn were sitting in the lobby of a retirement home. Mr. Steinberg, a widower himself, says to Joyce "For five dollars, I'll have sex with you on that rocking chair over there. For ten dollars, I' 11 have sex with you on that couch. But for twenty dollars, I'll take you to my room, light a few candles and give you a romantic evening of passion you'll never forget." Joyce considers this for a moment, then after digging through her purse, produces a twenty dollar bill. Mr. Steinberg says. "So, you want the romantic night in my room, eh?" To which Joyce replies "No, I want four times in the rocker!"

A guy from Tyson Foods arranges to visit the Pope. After receiving the papal blessing he whispers "Your Eminence, we have a deal for you. If you change The Lord's Prayer from give us this day our daily bread to give us this day our daily chicken, then we will donate $500 million dollars to the Church." The Pope replies by saying "That is impossible. The Prayer is the Word of the Lord and it must not be changed." "Well," says the Tyson man "we are prepared to donate 1 billion dollars to the Church if you change the Lord's Prayer from give us this day our daily bread to give us this day our daily chicken" Again the Pope replies "Impossible. The Prayer is the Word of the Lord and it must not be changed." Finally the Tyson guy says "This is our last offer. We will donate $5 billion to the church if you change the Lord's Prayer from give us this day our daily bread to give us this day our daily chicken and he leaves." The next day the Pope meets with the Holy College of Cardinals to say that he has some good news and some bad news. "The good news is that the Church has come into $5 billion. The bad news is that we are losing the Wonder Bread account!"

Seems an elderly gentleman had serious hearing problems for a number of years. He went to the doctor and the doctor was able to have him fitted for a set of hearing aids that allowed the gentleman to hear. The elderly gentleman went back in a month to the doctor and the doctor said "Your hearing's perfect, your family must he really pleased that you can hear again." To which the gentleman said "Oh, I haven't told them yet. I just sit around and listen to the conversations and I've already changed my will three times!"

It's the time of the French Revolution and they are doing their usual daily beheadings. Today they're leading a priest, an auditor and an engineer up to the guillotine. They ask the priest if he wants to be face up or face down when he meets his fate. The priest says that he would like to be face up so he'll be looking toward Heaven when he dies. They raise the blade of the guillotine, release it and it comes speeding down and suddenly stops just inches from his neck. Being devoutly religious they take this as divine intervention and release the priest. Next the auditor comes to the guillotine. He also decides to die face up hoping that he will be as fortunate as the priest. They raise the blade of the guillotine, release it, it comes speeding down and suddenly stops just inches from his neck. So they release the auditor as well. The engineer is next and he too decides to die facing up. They raise the blade of the guillotine and suddenly the engineer cries out: "Hey, I see what your problem is!"

I saw a lady at work today putting a credit card into her floppy drive and pulling it out very quickly. I inquired what she was doing and the lady explained that she was shopping on the internet and they asked for a credit card number, so she was using the ATM thingy on her computer.

One of our computer servers crashed and I was watching our new system administrator trying to restore it. He inserted a CD and needed to type a path name to a directory named "i386". He started to type it, paused, asking me "Where's the key for that line thing?" I asked what he was talking about and he said. "You know, that one that looks like an upside-down exclamation mark." I replied "You mean the letter "I" and he said, "Yeah, that's it!"

I recently saw a distraught young lady weeping beside her car. "Do you need some help?" I asked. She replied "I knew I should have replaced the battery in this remote door unlocker. Now I can't get into my car. Do you think that convenience store 2 blocks away would have a battery for this?" "Hmmm, I don't know, do you have an alarm on the car?" I asked. "No, just this remote thingy." she answered handing it and the car keys to me. As I took the keys and manually unlocked the door, I replied "Why don't you drive over there and check about those batteries, it's a long walk."

1st Person "Do you know anything about this fax-machine?"
2nd Person "A little, what's wrong?"
1st Person "Well, I sent a fax and the recipient called back to say all she received was a cover-sheet and a blank page. I tried it again, and the same thing happened."
2nd Person "How did you load the sheet?"
1st Person "It's a pretty sensitive memo and I didn't want anyone else to read it by accident, so I folded it so only the recipient would open it and read it."

Tech Support “What does the screen say now..”
Person “It says, ‘Hit ENTER when ready’.”
Tech Support “Well?”
Person “How do I know when it's ready?”

Several years ago we had an intern who was none too swift. One day he was typing and turned to a secretary and said. “I'm almost out of typing paper, what do I do?” “Just use copier machine paper” she told him. With that, the intern took his last remaining blank piece of paper, put it on the photocopier and proceeded to make five blank copies.

I was in a car dealership awhile ago when a large new motor home was towed into the garage. The front of the vehicle was in dire need of repair and the whole thing generally looked like an extra in the movie ‘Twister’. I asked the manager what had happened and he told me “The driver set the cruise control and then went in back to the kitchen to make a sandwich.”

Joan was the resident expert on the photocopy machine. One day there was a big backup. She went over to help and found that no one knew how to stop the copier from “punching” three holes down the side of each copy. She opened the paper tray, removed the three-hole paper and solved the problem.

New Corporate Buzz Words

Alpha Geek: The most knowledgeable technically proficient person in an office or work group. “Ask Larry, he's the Alpha Geek around here.

Assmosis: The process, by which some people seem to obtain advancement, by kissing up to the boss rather than working hard.

Blamestorming: Sitting around in a group discussing why a deadline was missed or a project failed, and who was responsible.

Body Nazis: Hard-core exercise and weight-lifting fanatics who look down on anyone who doesn't work out obsessively.

Chainsaw Consultant: An outside expert brought in to reduce the employee headcount leaving the top brass with clean hands.

Chips and Salsa: Chips is hardware and Salsa is software. “Well, first we have to figure out if the problem is in your chips or your salsa.”

Cube Farm: An office filled with cubicles.

Flight Risk: Used to describe employees who are suspected of planning to leave a company or department soon.

Going Postal: Euphemism for being totally stressed out and losing it. It makes reference to the unfortunate proclivity of some postal employees to go on shooting rampages at work.

Idea Hamsters: People who always seem to have their idea generators running.

Irritainment: Entertainment and media spectacles that are annoying but you find yourself unable to stop watching them. The O.J. trials were a prime example.

Mouse Potato: The online, wired generation's answer to the couch potato.

Percussive Maintenance: The fine art of whacking the crap out of an electronic device to get it to work again.

Prairie Dogging: When someone yells or drops something loudly in a cube farm and people's heads pop up over the walls to see what's going on.

Seagull Manager: A manager who flies in, makes a lot of noise, craps all over everything and then leaves.

SITCOMs: What yuppies turn into when they have children and one of them stops working to stay home with the kids. It is an acronym for **S**ingle **I**ncome **T**wo **C**hildren **O**ppressive **M**ortgage.

Stress Puppy: A person who seems to thrive on being stressed out and whiny.

Swiped Out: An ATM or credit card that has been rendered useless because the magnetic strip is worn away from extensive use.

Tourists: People who take training classes just to get a vacation from their jobs. “We had three serious students in class; the rest were just tourists.”

Treeware: Hacker slang for documentation or other printed material.

Uninstalled: Euphemism for being fired. Heard on the voicemail of a Vice President at a downsizing computer firm: “You have reached the number of an uninstalled Vice President. Please dial our main number and ask the operator for assistance.” See also Decruitment.

Vulcan Nerve Pinch: The taxing hand positions required to reach all the appropriate keys for certain commands. For instance, the warm re-boot for a Mac II computer involves simultaneously pressing the Control Key, the Command key, the Return key and the Power On key.

Xerox Subsidy: Euphemism for swiping free photocopies from one's workplace.

TRANSLATING MANAGEMENT SPEAK
Management Speak (MS): That's very interesting.
Translation (T): I disagree.

MS: I don't disagree.
T: I disagree.

MS: I don't totally disagree with you.
T: You may be right, but I don't care.

MS: You have to show some flexibility.
T: You have to do it whether you want to or not.

MS: We have all opportunity.
T: You have a problem.

MS: You obviously put a lot of work into this.
T: This is awful.

MS: In a perfect world.
T: Just get it working.

MS: Help me to understand.
T: I don't know what you're talking about, and I don't think you do either.

MS: You just don't understand our business.
T: We don't understand our business.

MS: You need to see the big picture.
T: My boss thinks it's a good idea.

MS: I appreciate your contribution.
T: Fuck you!

MS: We're going to follow a strict methodology here.
T: We're going to do it my way.

MS: We have unlimited resources.
T: You're working weekends.

MS: I didn't understand the e-mail you said you sent, can you give me a quick summary?
T: I still can't figure out how to start the e-mail program.

MS: Individual contributor.
T: Employee who does real work.

MS: Your project is on hold.
T: We've put a bullet in it.

MS: Wrong answer.
T: You didn't tell me what I wanted to hear.

MS: YOU needed to be more proactive.
T: You should have protected me from myself.

MS: I'd like your buy-in on this.
T: I want someone else to blame when this thing bombs.

MS: We want you to be the executive champion of this project.
T: I want to be able to blame you for my mistakes.

MS: We need to syndicate this decision.
T: We need to spread the blame around.

MS: We have to put on our marketing hats.
T: We have to put ethics aside.

MS: It's not possible. It's impractical. It won't work.
T: I don't know how to do it.

MS: It's a no-brainer.
T: It's a perfect decision for me to handle.

MS: I'm glad you asked me that.
T: Public relations has written a carefully phrased answer.

MS: I see you involved your peers in developing your proposal.
T: One person couldn't possibly come up with something this stupid.

MS: There are larger issues at stake.
T: I've made up my mind so don't bother me with the facts.

MS: I'll never lie to you.
T: The truth will change frequently.

MS: Our business is going through a paradigm shift.
T: We have no idea what you've been doing, but in the future we shall do something completely different.

MS: Value-added.
T: Expensive.

MS: The upcoming reductions will benefit the vast majority of employees.
T: The upcoming reductions will benefit me.

Two bees ran into each other. One asked the other how things were going. "Really bad," said the second bee "the weather has been really wet and damp and there aren't any flowers or pollen, so I can't make any honey." "No problem," said the first bee "just fly down five blocks, turn left and keep going until you see all the cars. There's a Bar Mitzvah going on and there are all kinds of fresh flowers and fresh fruit." "Thanks for the tip" said the second bee and flew away. A few hours later, the two bees ran into each other again and the first bee asked "How'd it go?" "Fine" said the second bee "it was everything you said it would be." "Uh, what's that thing on your head?" asked the first bee. "Oh that, it's my yarmulke," said the second bee "I didn't want them to think I was a wasp."

A man walks into an emergency room with two black eyes and a five iron wrapped tightly around his throat. Naturally the doctor asks him what happened. "Well, it was like this" said the man. "I was having a quiet round of golf with my wife when she sliced her hall into a pasture of cows. We went to look for it and while I was rooting around, I noticed one of the cows had something white at its rear end. I walked over, lifted up the tail and sure enough there was my wife's golf ball-stuck right in the middle of the cow's butt. That's when I made my mistake." "What did you do?" asked the doctor. "Well, I held up the tail and yelled to the missus, hey, this one sure looks like yours!"

Virus Alerts

Kenneth Starr Virus: Completely examines every aspect of your computer then compiles a complex report that discredits aspects of your computer.

Lewinsky Virus: Sucks all the memory out of your computer then e-mails everyone about what it did.

Ronald Reagan Virus: Saves your data, but forgets where it is stored.

Mike Tyson Virus: Quits after two bytes. Spits everything out.

Oprah Winfrey Virus: Your 300 MB hard drive suddenly shrinks to 100MB then slowly expands to 200 MB.

Doctor Kevorkian Virus: Deletes all old files.

Ellen Degeneres Virus: Disks can no longer be inserted.

Titanic Virus: Your whole computer goes down.

Disney Virus: Everything in your computer goes Goofy.

Prozac Virus: Screws up your RAM, but your processor doesn't care.

Joey Buttafuco Virus: Only attacks minor files.

Arnold Schwarzenegger Virus: Terminates zome viles, leaves, but it will be baaack:

Lorena Bobbit Virus: Reformats your hard drive into a 5 inch floppy, then discards it through Windows.

Viagra Virus: Makes a new hard drive out of an old floppy.

Clinton Virus: Gives you a 7 inch hard drive with no memory.

Don't You Hate it When...

You have to try on a pair of sunglasses with that stupid little plastic thing hanging in the middle of them.

The person behind you in the supermarket keeps running his cart into the back of your ankle.

The elevator stops on every floor and nobody gets on.

There's always a car riding on your tail when you're slowing down to find an address.

You open a can of soup and the lid falls in.

It's bad enough that you step in dog poop but you don't realize it until you walk across your living room rug.

The tiny red string on the Band-Aid wrapper never unrolls for you.

There's a dog in the neighborhood that barks at everything.

You can never put anything back in a box the way it came.

Three hours and three meetings after lunch you look in the mirror and discover a piece of parsley stuck to your front tooth.

You drink from a soda can into which someone has extinguished a cigarette.

There are always one or two ice cubes that won't pop out of the tray.

Your tire gauge lets out half the air while you are trying to get a reading.

You slice your tongue licking an envelope.

A station comes in brilliantly when you're standing near the radio but buzzes, drifts and spits every time you move away.

You wash a garment with a tissue in the pocket and the entire laundry comes out covered with lint.

The car behind you blasts its horn because you let a pedestrian finish crossing.

A piece of foil candy wrapper makes electrical contact with your filling.

You set the alarm on your digital clock for 7pm instead of 7am.

The radio station doesn't tell you who sang that song.

You rub on hand cream and can't turn the bathroom doorknob to get out.

People behind you on a supermarket line dash ahead of you to a counter just opening up.

You can't look up the correct spelling of a word in the dictionary because you don't know how to spell it.

Your glasses slide off your ears when you perspire.

You have to inform five different sales people in the same store that you're just browsing.

You had that pen in your hand only a second ago and now you can't find it.

You reach under the table to pick something off the floor and smash your head on the way up.

A blonde guy walks into a pharmacy and asks the young female assistant for some "anal deodorant." The young assistant tells the customer that they stock no such item, yet the customer says he purchased some just the other week. Blushing, the assistant goes and gets the owner who comes up to the customer and asks what he needs. "Some anal deodorant" replies the customer. The owner says that they do not stock such an item but the customer insists that they do, and that he just purchased some recently. In despair, the owner tells the customer to look around and try and find what he is referring to, so the customer looks around. After a short time he stops and picks up a stick of underarm deodorant and hands it to the owner. "This is underarm deodorant, what makes you think it is anal deodorant?" he says to the customer. The customer replies "Because on the back here it says push up bottom to use!"

Three older ladies were discussing the travails of getting older. One said "Sometimes I catch myself with a jar of mayonnaise in my hand in front of the refrigerator and can't remember whether I need to put it away, or start making a sandwich.” The second lady chimed in “Yes, sometimes I find myself on the landing of the stairs and can't remember whether I was on my way up or on my way down.” The third one responded “Well, I'm glad I don't have that problem knock on wood” as she rapped her knuckles on the table. She then told them “Oh that must be the door, I'll get it!”

Two men at a bar were getting pretty drunk when one of them notices a beautiful woman sitting in the corner. One says to the other “Gee, I'd really like to dance with that girl.” The other man replies “Well go ahead and ask her don't be a chicken shit.” So the man bravely approaches the lovely woman and says “Excuse me, would you be so kind as to dance with me?” Seeing the man is totally drunk the woman says “Right now I'm concentrating on matrimony and I'd rather sit than dance.” So the man humbly returns to his friend. “So what did she say?” asks the friend. The drunk responds “She said she's constipated on macaroni, and would rather shit in her pants.”

What's the difference between a Ritz cracker and a lesbian?
One is a snack cracker and the other is a crack snacker!
OR
One is a snack cracker and the other is a snatch cracker!

How to be a good Democrat

1. You have to believe the AIDS virus is spread because of a lack of federal funding.

2. You have to believe that the same teacher who can't teach 4th graders how to read is somehow qualified to teach those same kids about sex.

3. You have to believe that guns in the hands of law-abiding Americans are more of a threat than U.S. nuclear weapons technology in the hands of Chinese communists.

4. You have to believe that there was no art before Federal funding.

5. You have to believe that global temperatures are less affected by cyclical, documented changes in the earth's climate, and more affected by yuppies driving SUVs.

6. You have to be against capital punishment but support abortion on demand; in short, you support protecting the guilty and killing the innocent.

7. You have to believe that gender roles are artificial but being homosexual is natural.

8. You have to believe that businesses create oppression and governments create prosperity.

9. You have to believe that hunters don't care about nature but loony activists who've never been outside of Seattle do.

10. You have to believe that self-esteem is more important than actually doing something to earn it.

11. You have to believe the military, not corrupt politicians start war.

12. You have to believe the NRA is bad because it supports certain parts of the Constitution while the ACLU is good because it supports certain parts of the Constitution.

13. You have to believe that taxes are too low, but ATM fees are too high.

14. You have to believe that Margaret Sanger and Gloria Steinem are more important to our history than Thomas Jefferson, General Robert E. Lee or Thomas Edison.

15. You have to believe that standardized tests are racist but racial quotas and set-asides aren't.

16. You have to believe that the only reason socialism hasn't worked anywhere it's been tried is because the right people haven't been in charge.

MORE GREETING CARDS

I knew the day would come when you would leave me for my best friend. So here's his leash, water bowl and chew toys.

We have been friends for a very long time what's say we call it quits.

I'm so miserable without you, it's almost like you're here.

Congratulations on your new bundle of joy. Did you ever find out who the father was?

You are such a good friend that if we were on a sinking ship and there was only one life jacket, I'd miss you heaps and think of you often!

Your friends and family wanted to do something special for your birthday so we're having you put to sleep.

A doctor died and went to hell. He was met at the gate and told to stand in a room and wait for Satan. After 4 hours Satan finally appeared. The doctor was incensed. Poking his watch he said "How could you keep me waiting so long, I am an important man, I'm a doctor!" Satan replied "Doctors are a dime a dozen here in Hell but I'll tell you what, since you had to wait so long, I will give you a choice of which part of hell you will spend eternity in." Satan took the doctor down a hall and said "Here, I'll be back shortly, you can choose between Door #1 and Door #2. When I come back you can let me know where you want to be assigned."

The doctor opened Door #1 and inside was an Intensive Care Unit. Blood was spurting, alarms were going off and patients were coding. A man in the corner extubated himself as a woman in the center fell out of bed. The doctor quickly shut the door and said, “My God, I really am in Hell, I'd better check Door #2.” Behind Door #2 was a Medical Records Department. Unfinished charts stretched for miles with notations about delinquent history and physicals, message slips from Managed Care Case Managers filled a swimming pool sized bin, all marked Urgent. Inside physicians were dictating as sweat poured of their brows. The doctor shut the door and said “I don't know which one is worse.” Then he noticed another door off to the side. He opened it and inside was a tidy nurse's station. It was filled with nurses all were beautiful. They were busily making rounds with doctors, calling to obtain lab and x-ray results and they poured coffee and served donuts purchased with their own money. One doctor complained of a stiff neck and a nurse rubbed it for him. “Now this is more like it” the doctor thought as he closed the door. Satan came strolling back down the hall and said “Well, which have you decided on Door #1 or Door #2?” The doctor replied “Actually, I would like to go behind Door #3.” Well, that's not an option” said Satan. “But that's what I want” said the doctor. Satan replied “I'm sorry but you can't go in there. that's Hell for nurses.”

An Italian family is at the dinner table when the lather says to his oldest son, “Tony! Why you-a such a fat-a fuck?” Tony says, “Poppa, it's-a Mama's spaghetti. I can't-a stop-a eating it.” Poppa says “You should-a take-a smaller bites” Then Poppa says to his middle son. “Michael, why you-a such a fat-a fuck?” Michael says, “Poppa, it's-a Mama's lasagna I can't-a stop-a eating it, it's-a so good.” Poppa says “You should-a also take-a smaller bites.” Then Poppa says to his youngest son Alfredo “How you-a stay so slim-a and-a trim-a.” Alfredo says “It's-a so easy Poppa, I eat-a lots and lots of-a pussy.” Poppa says “Pussy, Pussy, that's-a taste like shit!”

Alfredo says "Poppa, you should-a take-a smaller bites!"

A husband, wife and a son walk into an ice-cream shop. The dad says "I'll have a chocolate." The wife says "I'll have a vanilla." Then the dad slaps his son in the back of the head and says "What do you want fat head?" The lady helping them says "Why did you hit him in the back of the head and call him fat head?" The husband says "There are three things in life a man wants: the first thing is a nice big truck. And you see that nice big truck sitting out there? That's my nice truck! The second thing in life a man wants is a nice big house. Have you seen that nice big house on top of the hill on College Street, that's my big house! The third thing in life a man wants is a nice tight pussy and I had that until fat head came along!"

A group of girlfriends is on vacation when they see a 5-story hotel with a sign that reads, "For Women Only." Since they were without their boyfriends or parents, they decide to go in. The Bouncer, a very attractive guy, explains to them how it works. "We have 5 floors, you go up floor by floor and once you find what you are looking for, you can stay there. It's easy to decide, since each floor has signs telling you what's inside." So they start going up, and on the first floor the sign reads "All the men here have it short and thin" The friends laugh and without hesitation move on to the next floor. The sign on the Second floor reads "All the men here have it long and thin." Still this wasn't good enough so the friends move up to the Third floor where the sign reads "All the men here have it short and thick." This was still another disappointment but knowing there are still 2 floors left, they move on to the next floor.
In the Fourth floor the sign was perfect. "All the men here have it long and thick." The women get all excited and are going in when they realize that there is one floor left. Wondering what they are missing, they go to the Fifth floor, where the sign reads "There are no men here. This floor was built only to prove that there is no way to please women."

A woman desperately looking for work goes into a toy factory and informs the personnel manager that she will take anything. The personnel manager hems and haws and finally says he has a low skill job on the "Tickle Me Elmo" line and nothing else. The woman happily accepts. He takes her down to the line, explains her duties, and tells her to start at 8:00 a.m. the next day. The next day at 8 :15 a.m. there's a knock at the personnel manager's door. The "Tickle Me Elmo" line manager starts ranting about the new hire. He screams that the assembly line is badly backed up. The personnel manager suggests that the supervisor show him the problem. They go to the assembly line, and sure enough, Elmos are backed up from here to kingdom come. The new hire is at the end of the line where she has an entire roll of the bright fabric used to make the Elmos and she has a big bag of marbles. They both watch her curiously as she cuts a little piece of fabric, takes 2 marbles and starts sewing them between Elmo's legs. The Personnel Manager is killing himself laughing and finally after pulling himself together, walks over to the new hire and says "I'm sorry, I guess you misunderstood my instructions yesterday. What you need to do is give Elmo two test tickles."

<u>I the penis, hereby request a raise in salary for the following reasons:</u>

1. I do physical labor.
2. I work at great depths.
3. I work head first.
4. I do not get weekends or public holidays off.
5. I work in a damp environment.
6. I don't get paid overtime or shift penalties.
7. I work in a dark workplace that has poor ventilation.
8. I work in high temperatures.
9. My work exposes me to contagious diseases.

The Response From The Administration: After assessing your request and considering the arguments you have raised, the administration rejects your request for the following reasons:

1. You do not work 8 hours straight.
2. You fall asleep on the job after hard work periods.
3. You do not always follow the orders of the management team.
4. You do not stay in your allocated position and often visit other areas.
5. You take a lot of non-scheduled breaks.
6. You do not take initiative, you need to be pressured and stimulated in order to start working.
7. You leave the workplace rather messy at the end of your shift.
8. You don't always observe safety measures, such as wearing the correct protective outfits.
9. You don't like working double shifts.
10. You sometimes leave your allocated position before you have completed the days work
11. And if that were not enough, you have been seen constantly entering and leaving the workplace carrying 2 suspicious looking bags.

One bright Saturday morning, Bob and his buddies are about to tee-off for their weekly game when Bob remembers he forgot to tell his wife about the repair man coming to look at the air conditioner. He excuses himself and quickly retreats to the club to make a call home. A sweet little voice answers on the second ring. “Hi, honey it's Daddy” says Bob, is mommy near the phone?” “No, Daddy. She's upstairs in the bedroom with Uncle Frank.” After a brief pause Bob says “But you haven't got an Uncle Frank honey!” “Yes I do and he's upstairs in the bedroom with Mommy.” “Okay then, here's what I want you do. Put down the phone, run upstairs and knock on the bedroom door and shout in to Mommy and Uncle Frank that Daddy's car's just pulled up in the driveway.” “Okay, Daddy!” A few minutes later the little girl comes hack to the phone crying. “Well, I did what you said Daddy.” “Well, what happened?” Bob asked. “Well Mommy jumped out of bed with no clothes on and ran around screaming, then she tripped over the rug and fell and I think she's really hurt bad." "Oh my God, what about Uncle Frank?" "He jumped out of bed with no clothes on too and he was all scared and he jumped out the back window into the swimming pool, but he must have forgotten that last week you took out all the water to clean it, so he hit the bottom of the swimming pool and I think he's dead." There is a long pause, then Bob says. "Swimming pool? Is this 854-7019?"

After having their 11th child, an Alabama couple decided that was enough, they could not afford a larger double wide. The husband goes to the doctor (who also treated mules) and told him that he and his wife didn't want to have anymore children. The doctor told him that there was a procedure called a vasectomy that could fix the problem. The doctor instructed him to go home, get a cherry bomb, light it, put it in a beer can, then hold the can up to his ear and count to 10. The Alabamian said to the doctor "I may not be the smartest man, but I don't see how putting a cherry bomb in a beer can next to my ear is going to help me." So, the couple drove to Georgia to get a second opinion. In Georgia, the doctor was just about to describe the procedure for a vasectomy when he read on the chart that they were from Alabama. So instead, the doctor also told the man to go home and get a cherry bomb, light it, place it in a beer can, hold it to his ear and count to 10. Figuring that both doctors couldn't be wrong, the man went home, lit a cherry bomb and put it in a beer can. He held the can up to his car and began to count. "l, 2, 3, 4, 5," at which point he paused, placed the beer can between his legs and resumed counting on his other hand....

The bartender was washing his glasses when an elderly Irishman came in and with great difficulty, hoisted his bad leg onto a barstool, pulled himself up painfully and asked for a sip of Irish whiskey. The Irishman looked down the bar and said. "Is that Jesus down there?" The bartender nodded and the Irishman told him to give Jesus an Irish whiskey too. The next patron was an ailing Italian with a hunched back and slowness of movement. He shuffled up to the barstool and asked for a glass of Chianti. He also looked down the bar and asked if that was Jesus sitting down there.

The bartender nodded and the Italian said to give Jesus a glass of Chianti. A third patron, a redneck, swaggered in dragging his knuckles on the floor and hollered "Barkeep, set me up a cold one. Hey, is that God's Boy down there?" The barkeep nodded, and the redneck told him to give Jesus a cold one too. As Jesus got up to leave, he walked over to the Irishman, touched him and said. "For your kindness, you are healed!" The Irishman felt the strength come back to his leg, and he got up and danced a jig to the door.

Then Jesus touched the Italian and said, "For your kindness you are healed!" The Italian felt his back straighten and he raised his hands above his head and did a flip out the door. Jesus walked toward the redneck but the redneck jumped back and exclaimed "Don't touch me, I'm drawin' disability!"

The mother-in-law stopped unexpectedly by the recently married couple's house. She rang the doorbell and stepped into the house only to find her daughter-in-law standing naked by the door. "What are you doing?" she asked. "I'm waiting for my husband to come home from work." "But, you're naked!" the mother-in-law exclaimed. "This is my love dress" the daughter-in-law explained.

"Love dress? But you're naked!" said the exasperated mother. "My husband loves me to wear this dress! It makes him happy and it makes me happy and I'd appreciate it if you would leave because he will be home from work any minute." The mother-in-law left in a huff but she couldn't stop thinking about the love dress so when she got home, she undressed, showered, put on her best perfume and waited by the front door. Finally her husband came home, walked in and saw her standing naked by the door. "What in the world are you doing?" he asked. "This is my love dress" she replied coyly. "Needs ironing!" he replied.

Q. What are two reasons why men die young?
A. Women and children.

<u>The Male Dictionary</u>
I'M GOING FISHING.
Translated: I'm going to drink myself dangerously stupid, stand by a stream with a stick in my hand, while the fish swim by in complete safety.

IT'S A GUY THING.
Translated: There is no rational thought pattern connected with it and you have no chance at all of making it logical.

CAN I HELP WITH DINNER.
Translated: Why isn't it already on the table.

UH HUH SURE HONEY or YES DEAR.
Translated: Absolutely nothing. It's a conditioned response.

IT WOULD TAKE TOO LONG TO EXPLAIN.
Translated: I have no idea how it works.

TAKE A BREAK HONEY, YOU'RE WORKING TOO HARD.
Translated: I can't hear the game over the vacuum cleaner.

THAT'S INTERESTING, DEAR.
Translated: Are you still talking?

YOU KNOW HOW BAD MY MEMORY IS.
Translated: I remember the theme song to 'F Troop', the address of the first girl I ever kissed and the vehicle identification numbers of every car I've ever owned, but I forgot your birthday.

I HEARD YOU.
Translated: I haven't the foggiest clue what you just said and

I'm hoping desperately that I can fake it well enough so that you don't spend the next 3 days yelling at me.

I WAS JUST THINKING ABOUT YOU, AND GOT YOU SOME ROSES.
Translated: The girl selling them on the corner was a real babe.

OH, DON'T FUSS, I JUST CUT MYSELF, IT'S NO BIG DEAL.
Translated: I have actually severed a limb, but will bleed to death before I admit that I'm hurt.

HEY, I'VE GOT MY REASONS FOR WHAT I'M DOING.
Translated: And I sure hope I think of some pretty soon.

I CAN'T FIND IT.
Translated: It didn't fall into my hands so I'm completely clueless.

WHAT DID I DO THIS TIME.
Translated: What did you catch me at

YOU KNOW I COULD NEVER LOVE ANYONE ELSE.
Translated: I'm used to the way you yell at me and realize it could be worse.

YOU LOOK TERRIFIC.
Translated: Oh, please don't try on one more outfit, I'm starving.

I'M NOT LOST. I KNOW EXACTLY WHERE WE ARE.
Translated: No one will ever see us alive again.

To be happy with a man, you must understand him a lot and love him a little. To be happy with a woman, you must love her a lot and try not to understand her at all.

Married men live longer than single men, but married men are a lot more willing to die.

Romance Math
Smart Man + Smart Woman = Romance
Smart Man + Dumb Woman = Affair
Dumb Man + Smart Woman = Marriage
Dumb Man + Dumb Woman = Pregnancy

Shopping Math
A man will pay $2 for a $1 item he needs.
A woman will pay $1 for a $2 item that she doesn’t need.

A woman worries about the future until she gets a husband.
A man never worries about the future until he gets a wife.
A successful man is one who makes more money than his wife can spend.
A successful woman is one who can find such a man.

Any married man should forget his mistakes. There's no use in two people remembering the same thing.

Men wake up as good-looking as they went to bed.
Women somehow deteriorate during the night.

A woman marries a man expecting him to change but he doesn't.
A man marries a woman expecting that she won’t change and she does.

Married men do not live longer than single men, it just feels that way.

Q. Why do men die before women?
A. They chose to.

There are two times a man does not understand a woman, before marriage and after marriage.

The US Treasury has just announced that it will sell 3 new different types of government bonds:
1. The Al Gore Bond which has no interest.
2. The Monica Lewinsky Bond which has no maturity.
3. The Bill Clinton Bond, which has no principle.

One afternoon, Sue was in the backyard hanging the laundry when an old, tired-looking dog wandered into the yard. Sue could tell from his collar and well-fed belly that he had a home. But when she walked into the house he followed her in, sauntered down the hall and fell asleep in a corner. An hour later, the dog went to the door and Sue let him out. The next day he was back. He resumed his position in the hallway and slept for an hour. This continued for several weeks. Curious, Sue pinned a note to his collar which read "Everyday your dog comes to my house for a nap." The next day the dog arrives with a little note pinned to his collar "He lives in a home with ten children and he's trying to catch up on his sleep."

<u>SEXUAL RIDDLES</u>
Q. What do you say to a virgin when she sneezes?
A. Goes-in-tight!

Q. What did Cinderella do when she got to the ball?
A. Gagged!

Q. What do you call a man who cries while he masturbates?
A. A tearjerker.

Q. Define Egghead.
A. What Mrs. Dumpty gives to Humpty.

Q. How do you piss off Winnie the Pooh?
A. Stick your finger in his honey.

Q. Why are cowgirls bow legged?
A. Cowboys like to eat with their hats on.

Q. What's the definition of a teenager?
A. God's punishment for copulation.

Q. Why should you use a stealth condom?
A. She'll never see you Cuming.

Q. How is a woman like a road?
A. Both have manholes.

Q. What's the definition of a vagina?
A. The box a penis comes in.

Q. What two words will clear out a men's restroom?
A. Nice Dick!

Q. What do you call a truckload of vibrators?
A. Toys for Twats.

Q. Why do we have orgasms?
A. How else would we know when to stop?

Q. What's the definition of in the ball park?
A. When your balls are slapping up against her ass you're definitely in the ball park!

Q. What does Kodak film have in common with condoms?
A. Both capture the moment.

Q. Mom's have Mother's day and Dad's have Father's Day but what do single guys have?
A. Palm Sunday.

Q. What do you call five naked men sitting on each others shoulders?
A. A scrotum pole!

Q. What's the ultimate insult?
A. When you are masturbating and your hand falls asleep.

Q. What do dildos and soy beans have in common?
A. They are both used as meat substitute.

Q. What do you call kids born in whorehouses?
A. Brothel sprouts.

Q. How do crazy people go through the forest?
A. They take the psycho path.

Q. How do you get holy water?
A. You boil the hell out of it.

Q. What do fish say when they hit a concrete wall?
A. Dam!

Q. What do Eskimos get from sitting on the ice too long?
A. Polaroids.

Q. What do you call cheese that isn't yours?
A. Nacho cheese.

Q. What do you get from a pampered cow?
A. Spoiled milk.

Q. What's the difference between a bad golfer and a bad skydiver?
A. A bad golfer goes whack, damn. A bad skydiver goes damn, whack.

Q. What do you get when you cross a snowman with a Vampire?
A. Frostbite.

Q. What lies at the bottom of the ocean and twitches?
A. A nervous wreck.

Q. What is the difference between roast beef and pea soup?
A. Anyone can roast beef.

Q. Why don't blind people go sky diving?
A. Because it scares the guide dog.

Q. What kind of coffee did they serve on the Titanic?
A. Sanka

Q. What's the difference between a Harley and a Hoover?
A. The location of the dirt bag.

Q. Why does a pilgrim's pants always fall down?
A. Because they wear their belt buckle on their hat.

Q. Why do black men always have red eyes after sex?
A. from the pepper spray

Q. Why did the Mexicans fight so hard to get into the Alamo?
A. They thought it was a welfare office.

Q. What do you call a Mexican mechanic?
A. A Lubricano.

Q. How can you tell an Italian tire?
A. Dego through snow, dego through ice, dego through mud and when they go flat they go wop wop wop.

Q. What do you call a Mexican baptism?
A. A bean dip.

Q. What is a Mexican fortune cookie?
A. A taco with a welfare check in it.

Q. Why don't Mexicans barbeque?
A. Because the beans fall through the grill.

Q. Why do Mexicans drive low riders?
A. It makes it easier to pick the lettuce.

Q. How do we know Adam was not black?
A. Did you ever try and take away a rib from a black man.

Q. What are three things you can't give a black man?
A. A black eye, a fat lip and a job.

Q. How do you baby sit a black kid?
A. Wet his lips and stick him to the wall.

Q. How do you baby sit a Samoan kid?
A. Put Velcro on the ceiling and hang him by his hair.

Q. Why do black men always have sex on their mind?
A. They have pubic hair on their heads.

Q. Why do blacks have large nostrils?
A. That is where God held them when he painted them.

Q. Why are black men black everywhere except the palms of their hands and the soles of their feet?
A. That is where God told them to assume the position when he when he painted them OR everybody has a little good in them.

Q. Why do Jews have large nostrils?
A. Free air.

Q. How do you know Jesus Christ was Irish?
A. He thought his mom was a virgin, his mom thought her son was God, he trained as a carpenter, was unemployed, he lived at home until he was 30 and he was always hanging out with his 12 drinking buddies.

Q. What is another name for spaghetti?
A. Ginny Wop Slop.

Q. There is a Mexican and a Black in a car, who's driving?
A. The police officer.

Q. What do you call a black man in a three piece suit.
A. The defendant.

Q. Why do gay men grow mustaches?
A. To hide their stretch marks.